VL 6⁵⁹
YE

At the
Cross

The Napoleon Kaufman Story

Jimmie Hand
as Told By Napoleon Kaufman

cWc
Crucified With Christ Publishing
San Ramon, California

Contents

Acknowledgements

I would like to thank all those people who helped make this book possible. Without them it just would not have happened. Thank you all!

First, I want to thank Napoleon Kaufman for his inspiration in writing this book. Working with him, listening to him, in person, on the phone and by tape was a daily Bible study for me.

And thanks to Nicole Kaufman for all her help.

To Al Moak, my editor who did another outstanding job as usual. Thanks again!

To Freda Gregory Hand, my loving wife of 33 years who helped me find just the right words when I was stumped.

To Craig Long with the public relations department of the Oakland Raiders for supplying me everything I needed to know about the team and thanks for the great pictures.

And Lisa Center, Program Coordinator, Media relations form the University of Washington. Thanks Lisa for all the great articles and pictures.

Jonathan Gullery, for designing the cover and the book and much other help.

To Ron Johnson of RJ Communications in New York for doing such a great job of printing.

Preface

It had only been three days since I mailed a copy of my book *Isaac Bruce/ Family, Faith and the Final Touchdown* along with a proposal to Napoleon Kaufman of the Oakland Raiders about the possibility of writing his story.

You can't begin to understand my surprise when they phone rang and I heard, "Jimmie, this is Napoleon." Right! and I am Julius Caesar. No, I didn't say that, but I was taken aback I have to admit.

It's not that I have not been used to speaking with super star athletes on the telephone, because for the past thirty four years I had made my living as a Commercial Sports Agent and have had the privileged of working with many of the great ones, but for some reason this was different.

When I started writing just five years ago as therapy in my battle with cancer I never really dreamed that one-day I might be published. But now this is my third book and if Napoleon and I agreed on one thing, and we agreed on many things it was that we wanted his story and my writing to be to the glory of God.

I'm going on sixty-four years of age now and have come to the conclusion that that old saying, "Only what is done for Christ will last" really rings true. We both wanted the book to be informative for Napoleon's football fans, plus we wanted people to see what a walk with Jesus Christ can mean to a person no matter the age.

It's been two months now since that first conversation with Napoleon, and we have had many enjoyable conversations since, both in person and on the phone, and each time I speak with him I am amazed at how God is using this young man. His knowledge and recall of the Word of God, his insight into spiritual matters, is that of a person who has spent years in study and the work of God, but he just turned twenty - eight years old.

His desire, no, his insistence is that his leaving professional football at the height of his career be played down and the fact that the Lord God almighty called him to preach the gospel be the featured part of this story.

If you enjoy this book, please pass it on or tell a friend about it. It'll be great, when we all get to Heaven, to sit around and talk about this little book about a talented football player who put down the tools of professional football at the foot of the Cross of Christ to spread the Gospel!

Chapter 1

The Early Years

Napoleon's childhood had not been easy. Oh there were the fun times, the football and all the excitement that it brought to him, but being raised by a single mom whose life was filled with problems of her own, and with no husband around, all carried over to a young Napoleon.

Napoleon was born in Kansas City, Missouri on June 7, 1973. His father Napoleon II and his mother split up when he was just over one year old, and he moved with his mother to the small town of Lompoc on the central coast of California. (Lompoc is pronounced "Lom Poke" not "Lom Pock.") It's a neat little town, not too big, not too small. His grandfather and other members of his mother's family had lived in the area for quite awhile. His grandfather was in the Air Force stationed at Vandenberg Air Force Base.

Lompoc was fun for young Napoleon, and because he was an only child he soon developed a lot of friendships with kids from all over town. When he was about ten or eleven he hung out with some good buds like Tony Barber, Moose Mau, and Marshall Emerson, and they could find fun about anywhere.

They all started to play football about the same time, and that was their main interest . . . football. He and Moose Mau would continue to play together through high school with Moose playing outside linebacker on those great Lompoc teams. Unfortunately football was pretty nearly Napoleon's only interest. In fact it just seemed that when he wasn't playing football he was getting into some kind of trouble.

He wasn't an angry kid. He was a happy go lucky guy, but aggressive. Looking back at some of his Pop Warner football tapes he even now sees this little kid slamming other kids all over the place, and then he realizes "that little kid is me!" He can hardly believe it.

From the time he was eleven until he was about thirteen he experienced some of his toughest times. His mom had gone through some really difficult health problems and even battled an addiction to methadone, from which the Lord later delivered her. Even though she provided for him as best she could, times were tough.

Running with a couple of street gangs that went around town doing bad things was just one of his problems. Getting kicked out of school a number of times, he was finally sent to reform school and then even juvenile hall. At one point he was kicked out of Lompoc middle school and sent to Casa Floral, a reform school, and he had to have one hundred days there of good behavior there before they would let him return to the middle school.

School wasn't that hard for Napoleon, but he didn't care for the lessons. He went to school to be with his friends. It was more of a social thing for him. He thought of school as a place to play. Not having much of an attention span contributed to his problems.

If it hadn't been for football only God knows where he might have ended up. But God kept using football like a life preserver. In the time of trouble, football was there just in time. And God had sent guardian angles to look out for him, men like his uncle Tony White, Coaches Ron Mau in Pop Warner, Dick Barrett at Lompoc High School and Al Lavan his running back coach at the University of Washington.

There were other poor people in Lompoc, but to Napoleon it always seemed like he was at the bottom of the pile. It was this poverty factor plus no real Godly instruction in the home, that contributed to his getting into trouble, trouble and more trouble.

Also being small for his age meant he had to show everyone how "bad" he was, so he was always getting into fights. Stealing was another thing that kept him in hot water. All he wanted was to have things other kids his age had, but there was never money for those things at his place. There was hardly even money for a place at all. They were always on the threshold of eviction from the small apartments that he shared with his mother because of this they never lived in the same place for very long.

It's difficult enough even for two parents to raise a child these days, but his mother was alone in the parenting business, and there were additional burdens. Most of the time welfare was the only income they had except when his mother could find a low - paying part - time job.

He was very close to his mother especially when he was young. He always loved her and felt close to her even though their existence was a rough one.

Discipline was not Lajuana Kaufman's strong suit. Napoleon tells a funny story about a time he was with his mother at one of her friend's house. Napoleon said something mean to the friend. His mother took him into the bathroom and gave him a spanking. As he was walking back out from the bathroom Napoleon said, "That didn't hurt." Needless to say that didn't sit well with his mother and she gave him a little shove and he flopped over backwards, "you know, like Dennis Rodman does when he's trying to draw a foul. Boy did I milk that little bitty cut. You would have thought I was dying." That was the last spanking he got from his mother.

But his father could give a spanking!

Probably the best word to describe Napoleon III 's relationship with his father, Napoleon II, would be "awkward." We need to keep in mind that his father stayed in Kansas City after he was born when his mother moved to California. They moved when Napoleon was only a year and a half old and it was not until he was nine years old that he would again see his father. That was a long time between fatherly visits.

When he was nine he went back to Kansas City to stay with his father, but it didn't last long. The snow, which he had never seen before, and his father's spankings were about all he remembered about Kansas City.

He learned that his dad's spankings were not like his mothers. Napoleon II was a construction worker and a body builder and a very strong man. Napoleon III got the first taste of a real spanking one day after he got expelled from school for fighting, and he knew right then he didn't want any more of that.

But after a few months, Napoleon went back to Lompoc to live with his mother, and over the next ten years an occasional telephone call from his father was the only contact that they had with each other.

Then in his freshman year at the University of Washington the Huskies went to the Rose Bowl to play Michigan, and once again his father was there. Not having seen him for all those years, and then, all of a sudden . . . boom here's dad. Again the meeting was . . . awkward to say the least.

After Napoleon joined the Raiders he was able to see his father at least once a year when Oakland traveled back to KC to play the Chiefs. Only after he had asked Jesus to come into his heart and forgive him for his sins was he able to forgive his father and to ask his father to forgive him.

A GLIMPSE AT NAPOLEON'S HEART:

I can't begin to tell you how important a father is to a family. I know because I never had a day-to-day, live in father. I CAN tell you how hard it is on a youngster to NOT have a father around, because that was the life I knew.

When there is no male role model in the immediate family a kid seems to wander his own way, and I was like that. I hung out with some guys that I should have stayed clear of. I even joined a couple of gangs along the way. Kids fool themselves into thinking that gangs will fill their need for a family—— and to some degree they do. But the influences that gangs have are for bad and will eventually lead to destruction.

The need of a loving father is something special, and when you're growing up and seeing other kids going here or doing this or that with their dads, or when you come to school on Monday mornings and hear about all the great things the guys did with their fathers it makes you feel like an outcast and that's not a good feeling for any youngster.

If you don't have a dad you can just forget the father-son dinners or father-son outings. I knew that on school "parent days" I would be one of those kids that shared someone else's dad. That's embarrassing for a kid.

I didn't know what it meant to have a father in the home, much less a godly father. That was why it was so hard for me to understand the concept of a loving heavenly Father. How could I? I had no one to show me first hand what a father-son relationship was all about. I think that when I finally grasped what God had done for me in giving His only Son to die for me, that it was then that I knew for the first time what a true father-son relationship was. Praise God!

I am thankful for my Uncle Tony who did as much for me as any man, and for my Grandmother, whose name was Barbara. She has gone to be with the Lord now, but bless her heart, she was my anchor. She was the stabilizing force in our family. If I needed something or if I was hungry, I could always go to her house and she would take care of my needs. My Uncle Tony would be there. It was a place of refuge.

It was my Uncle Tony who introduced me to football when I was seven years old. I remember the day he bought me a new pair of football cleats and socks and then took me down and signed me up and paid my fees to play Pop Warner football. He was one that I could always look to in time of trouble. He was just like my Grandmother, a real refuge.

Another man who was very influential in my life was my Pop Warner coach, Ron Mau. He was father to my best friend, Moose Mau. Mr. Mau was my first football coach and throughout my life he has played an important part in any success I've attained. Later on, as I started to get into trouble, I was sent to reform school. Guess who my reform school teacher was? Right! It was Mr. Mau! He helped straighten me out and put me on the right road, and I stayed there for a while.

But as loving as Uncle Tony was, or Coach Barrett, or Mr. Mau and many other adults that have been in my life, they just couldn't take the place of my real father, try as they might. Boys and girls need both of their parents; it's as simple as that. That's the way God planned it, and nothing less will do.

I know there are many loving mothers out there who have had to become both mother and father to their children, whether through the death of a father or just his leaving, and they do wonderful jobs. The burden is unbelievable for that single mom. Take a minute to think what it must be like for them. There's never enough money for the necessities of life much less for the frills. How those mom's hearts must break when they continually have to say no to their children for the simple things in life.

My heart goes out to them, and we all should remember to help them and to pray for them whenever we can.

If you are a father and you have abdicated your position of leadership in your home to your wife because you think she prays better than you do or that she is more spiritual than you are, you need to change that attitude. God placed you as head of your home for a reason, and no excuse you can come up with will change that. Take that leadership and see how God will reward your effort, Take Him at His word!

You, through Jesus Christ are the covering for your family! You are to love, nurture, protect, provide for, and yes discipline your children. As God loves us He chastens us, so if you love your children you must see that they are raised in the ways of the Lord and that means godly discipline.

Not having a father in the home as a role model has left me to look to the scriptures to learn how to be a loving, caring husband and father and thank God, it's all right there in the Word.

Thank you Abba Father!

THE BIBLE TELLS US:

Galatians 4: 6-7
"Because you are sons, God sent the Spirit of his Son into our hearts, the Spirit who calls out '*Abba*, Father." So you are no longer a slave, but a son, and since you are a son, God has made you an heir."

Proverbs 13:1
"A wise son heeds his father's instruction."

2 Corinthians 6:18
"I will be a Father to you, and you will be my sons and daughters, says the Lord Almighty."

Chapter 2

The Blessing Zone

From the time Napoleon started playing Pop Warner football at age seven it was obvious to everyone who saw him play that he was something special. The very first time they put the football in his hands and told him to run, he ran for a touchdown. One touchdown after another—-it was sooo easy for him. He would catch himself laughing as he ran away from the other kids. God may have made him small but He sure made him fast!

He didn't realize just how fast he was until he started playing with other kids, it didn't matter whether they were playing football or tag he could outrun them all. When they would play pickup games in the park he was able to run faster that any of the other kids.

Ron Mau, Moose Mau's father, was a man that would leave a lasting impression on young Napoleon and it all started when "Little Nip's" Uncle Tony asked Coach Mau if he would give his nephew a shot at making his Pop Warner pee - wee football team. Tony had played years earlier for Mau and he knew he would give the little guy a fair chance.

Mau remembers well, "Everyone in town was aware of Napoleon's speed even at that age, but he was just this little kid, really small, very fragile looking and he wasn't very coordinated when he first started playing football. In fact he had trouble fielding the tailback pitches, but he sure could run!"

This was all new to Napoleon but he took to football like a duck takes to water and each year he improved in some aspect of his game. "At first he was afraid to run up the middle, he figured the fastest and safest way into the end zone was around the end but by his second season he was going inside like a fullback, and loving the contact. Napoleon had always been strong," Coach Mau recalled, "I'm sure it was his strength that got him to where he is today."

"He was a neat kid, so much fun to be around. He would get to practice every day about a half an hour earlier than the other kids and always with a good attitude. We'd walk out on the football field together, him with his arm around me and mine on his shoulder. And if you had seen the circumstances that made up his home life environment . . . you would wonder how anyone could have made it from that. It was horrible but he's something special!" Mau said.

"He was so creative! It was about the time he was in the fourth grade that I just knew he was going to be someone, do something whether sports, acting or singing, I just knew he was destined for something. I remember he used to lead the team around the field for warm-ups by doing a chant that he had made up, much like a marine drill sergeant with the other kids singing back to him. Here's this little guy jumping around and waving his arms like the leader of the band, it was hilarious."

Running fast came as easy as walking to him. His God - given speed was something that would take him a long way to many places and give him many opportunities.

Track also was much like football, easy for him. Again that speed came through. It was in middle school that he got his first look at track. This was a different kind of running than in football - where you run, stop on a dime, change direction, cut, run, move, run —- in track it was just run straight ahead as fast as you can.

By the time he got to high school at Lompoc High School he was starting to get some real track coaching from Coach Warren. It took him a little while to develop his own technique, but once he got things down it all fell into place. He was running the 100 and 200 meters, along with the long jump and he ran the relays.

By his junior year he was feeling pretty good about his chances in track, but never in his wildest dreams was he prepared for what he accomplished. On a hot spring day in 1990, his junior season, the Braves went to southern California for the state meet at El Camino College in Torrance, California and he was up to the challenge, winning both the 100 and 200 meter state championships. Not bad for someone who was just getting the feel of things!

Track and football came easy alright, but academics were a different matter. Sometimes he did very well in class if he happened to like the class and it kept his interest, but in the classes he didn't care for he did poorly.

Being an only child, when he got to school with all the other kids he just thought it was time to play.

Fortunately, when he was pretty young he had one teacher in particular that he really liked, Mrs. Jackson. She was a friend of his mom's, and was aware of his circumstances, and she sort of took him under her wing. "I'll never forget Mrs. Jackson," says Napoleon. She also brought so much needed discipline into his life.

One of his problems in school was that his attention span was short, And he certainly wasn't self -motivating when it came to schoolwork.

Sometimes he got into fights just to prove that he was tough, because he was smaller than most of the guys. One of his coaches remembered that "He wasn't a bully, but he did have a short fuse." Only later did he realize that fighting never solves anything but only makes things worse.

At age eleven he was baptized at the Grace Temple Baptist church by Pastor Dan Tullis and things started to become confusing for him. Even at that age God was working on his life even in all that sin and disobedience.

A Glimpse at Napoleon's Heart:

It's when we are in the Blessing Zone that we have to be careful. It's at the time when the enemy outside has been defeated and we are feeling warm and cozy with God that we have to be careful that the inner man doesn't rear up his ugly head and try to do us in. That inner man can be a stronger force than any outward enemy!

That inner man can knock us down in ways we couldn't imagine could happen to a born-again believer . . ." He'll tell you, "I know you messed up. I know you got knocked down . . . but I tell you Get up——Get up! I know you feel like quitting, but you have to get up——GET UP! You have to overcome it! You have to OVERCOME it! You've got to fight him to stay alive.

Jesus defeated the devil on Calvary. But I've got to deal with this inner man that keeps trying to get me. I've got to deal with this man that keeps trying to wage war against my soul. He keeps trying to take me down. I gotta stay alive! Some of you readers know what I'm taking about.

So, as God begins to take us into this place of blessing, where he shuts the enemy's mouth and we begin to enter into a place of intimacy with God, there's one thing we've got to watch out for. It's such a place of rest within ourselves that we fail to realize that God is still doing a work within us and he wants to complete this work until we're completely transformed into the image that is pleasing to Him, which is Jesus Christ.

And I recognize that all of my goodness is as filthy rags, but what He can do in and through me is the thing that matters. These are the things that are going to please Him. When I am so taken up with who He is, so transformed by His glory. Then I will please Him.

My charge to you my reader friends is to tell you that as God has abundantly blessed you, as He has taken you through your the wilderness journey, you need to stay close to Him. It isn't always easy. You have to overcome, and you can do it! He has brought you into a place in which you're getting into the flow.

I know when He takes us into that Blessing Zone that it can be a dangerous place. Remember to say "It's YOU Master." "It's YOUR power and YOUR strength that causes us to overcome." And when

You take us to that place of rest Lord Jesus we've got to remember not to loose our ground. I know it's a dangerous place but it's Your hearts' desire that we are there.

We have to stay true to you and keep that intimacy with You. Are we going to study the Word like we know we should and get it into our hearts so that we are transformed into what it says? Are we going to have the kind of prayer life that You want us to have in which we pray for our families and unsaved loved ones in a way that reaches heavens gates?

God has given us the best in His son Jesus Christ, and we must remember to give Him our best and be faithful to the end.

THE BIBLE TELLS US:

2 Timothy 2:15
"Study to show thyself approved, a workman who does not need to be ashamed and who correctly handles the word of truth."

Matthew 9:38
". . .the harvest is plentiful but the workers are few."

Romans 8:28
"And we know that in all things God works for the good of those who love him, who have been called according to his purpose."

Deuteronomy 7:9

" Know therefore that the Lord your God is God; He is the faithful God, keeping his covenant of love to a thousand generations of those who love him and keep his commandments."

Deuteronomy 8:2-3
"Remember how the Lord your God led you all the way in the desert these forty years, to humble you and to test you in order to know what was in your heart, whether or not you would keep His commands. He humbled you, causing you to hunger and then feeding you with manna neither you nor your fathers had known, to teach you man does not live on bread alone but on every word that comes from the mouth of the Lord."

Chapter 3

Walk in Glory!

Lompoc High school was a good school steeped in lots of tradition. Napoleons' four years as a Brave was overall an enjoyable time, especially the sports. The whole town supported the teams. When Lompoc played their games on Friday nights at Huyck Stadium the noisy crowd filled the stadium. On the road there was always a large group that followed their team wherever they played.

In his freshman year Napoleon weighed only one hundred and thirty-five pounds but he saw action on the freshman team. It was during this freshman year that people were to find out just how fast he really was. There was a track meet that first year when the Braves went to a league meet, and Napoleon had to race against a senior, a guy by the name of William Henry who was a state qualifying huddler and a speedster with a reputation. He was fast- but not quite fast enough. Napoleon beat him in the 100 meters to win the league championship.

It was Dick Barrett, his high school football coach, who took notice of this little speedster, and for his sophomore year he was moved up to the varsity. Barrett soon became a father-like figure to his young gladiator, and has remained a father-figure throughout the years. "He was like a father figure to me. He was there when my dad wasn't . . .at 14or 15, you need a dad around. He was always there, pushing me and staying after me."

Barrett first met Napoleon when he was in his remedial English class his freshman year at Lompoc. "He was just a goofy little freshman," Barrett remembers. "I moved him out of my remedial class when I saw the drive he had. He settled down and began to learn."

Napoleon's sophomore season was a tough one. Getting off to a bad start, the team was one and seven with Napoleon playing wingback. Barrett knew he had to do something to save the season so he switched Napoleon to tailback to better utilize his speed and quickness, and sure enough, the move paid off as his team made it to the state semi-finals! The shifty little tailback rushed for one thousand yards and let the people of California know there was a player in a small town on the central coast that they hadn't heard the last of.

By Napoleon's junior year Barrett had built a powerhouse team that went 13-1 and finished second in the state. Serra High School out of Los Angeles beat the Braves in the championship game but not because the Lompoc tailback had a bad game. Quite the contrary, he rushed for 167 yards and scored four touchdowns. He ran a kickoff back for one touchdown in an awesome game that some say was one of the best high school football games ever played in California. The final score was 34-31.

It was the first time Napoleon had played in front of a really large crowd, and he seemed to thrive on it. To him it was just like any other game. This seemed to be his secret to success throughout his football career, never too high, never to low, just staying on an even keel. He rushed for 2000 yards and scored 39 touchdowns and was named to the all-CIF team that season to end a great junior year.

As well as things were going on the athletic fields trouble continued to haunt him in school. That year he took the SAT for the first time and failed it. He was really down but Coach Barrett wasn't a man to let him sit and dwell on his failures. He sat Napoleon down and talked to him like a Dutch uncle. He said, "Napoleon; football is your ticket out of this little town. You can be what ever you want to be, but you have to stop this foolishness and apply yourself."

"That summer I had him take an algebra course and a course in SAT (Scholastic Aptitude Test) preparation. He went from 560 on the test to 710 and that was from May to October." The NCAA requires 700 to be eligible to play a sport. The dramatic improvement was viewed with such suspicion that documentary evidence was kept on hand to show that he had indeed taken the test and the scores were legitimate. If his 2.1 grade point average wasn't very impressive it sure was when added to a 4.31 second forty- yard dash.

Napoleon took to heart what his mentor had said, and took that summer course in how to pass the SAT. The day the results came in the mail he was at his mother's place. He opened the letter in doubt, but when he saw the score and it said that he had passed he couldn't believe it! He ran as fast as he could, probably breaking a world record in getting to Coach Barrett's office to show him the results.

The look on the coach's face made it all worthwhile. Barrett always beloved in Napoleon and wasn't going to let him blow his big chance. Coach Barrett was an encourager. He didn't do a lot of screaming and hollering. He just told his players to go out there and do the very best they could and everything else would take care of itself.

By his senior year Napoleon was up to 175 pounds, and that team went 13 and 2 and beat Arroyo Grande High School for the CIF championship. That year he rushed for 1960 yards on 207 carries for unbelievable 9.5 yards per carry and along the way he scored 28 touchdowns. He also scored three times on punt returns, twice on pass receptions and once on a kick-off for a total of 34 touchdowns.

He finished his high school career with 5,146 rushing yards, 68 touchdowns and 520 points, all among the top ten in CIF history.

After that great season he was chosen to play in two high school all-star games during the summer following his senior year. The prestigious North-South Shrine game pitted the best high school players in northern California against the best in southern California.

The game was held in the Rose Bowl. It would be his first trip to that great stadium, but not his last. He had a pretty good game to say the least as he put up big numbers and was named the MVP for the game. Next he played in the Santa Barbara County High School all-star game and had another sensational outing, winning the MVP award again.

Winning the 100 and 200 - meter state championships in his junior year was at that time, the highlight of his young sports career, but being named the outstanding high school football player in California his senior year was his proudest moment. He was named to many high school all-American teams such as Parade Magazines all-Americans, USA Today first team all-American, he was one of three players to get a perfect ten score in "The Best of the West," but it was that California MVP that he cherished the most.

From his sophomore year on he was heavily recruited by colleges all over. Washington considered him the top prospect in the country. It was a little heady when the letters first started to roll in but now that he had passed the SAT he would be eligible to take a full scholarship to about any university he chose.

USC and its famed tailback tradition with guys like Marcus Allen, O.J. Simpson, Ricky Bell, Mike Garrett (and the list went on with guys who had played that position for the Trojans) was something that first appealed to Napoleon, but after he visited the school he felt like he wasn't ready to go from a small country town to the heart of the inner city. It just didn't feel right to him.

USC, Arizona, Colorado, and an unofficial visit to UCLA were all stops on his travel agenda, but after his trip to Seattle and the University of Washington he had all he needed to make up his mind. He cancelled one last scheduled trip to the University of Nebraska.

He was about to get out of the little town that he liked so much and head out into the big world.

A GLIMPSE AT NAPOLEON'S HEART:

God tells us that He's going to raise up a generation to walk in His ways. We must walk in the Spirit. I don't know about you but I'm tired of struggling with the same old things over and over again. I want to walk in glory. I want to walk in the spirit daily. I want to walk in power. I'm tired of struggling with this and struggling with that. Man, I want to walk in glory! We're GOING to walk in glory. We're GOING to walk in glory!

But I believe that if we are going to walk in glory then we've got to allow God to do those things that he desires to do in our hearts. He's going to move our hearts and passions away from earthly things. We aren't friends of this world. If we're friends with someone it means that we have something in common with them. The Bible says "I've been born from above. I don't have anything in common with this world. The Bible says if any man be in Christ he is a new creation. Old things are passed away and all things become new.

Now I'm beginning to accept who I am in God because I have been born from above, and as a result I'm going to walk according to kingly principals, in submission to the kingship of almighty God. That's the difference that people are going to see, and it's going to draw them to the church when they see that we're walking and demonstrating the kingdom of God.

I want to challenge you readers because I believe that some of you, of this generation, are having God place a spear and a sword in your hand that you might do battle, that you might wage war against those things that have come against the church, things that try to hinder who we should be, and who God says we should be. And as a result of that, God is going to make a perpetual covenant with you. And it's not only going to affect you but it's going to affect your children and your children's children.

So you will have an inheritance that goes far beyond a new car and a big house, or some fleeting worldly fame but rather will have something that'll enable you to say when you are finally face to face with our Lord, "You know what Jesus? My father, he left me an inheritance that went far beyond anything natural. He taught me about a relationship with YOU. He taught me how to walk with You and talk with YOU. He taught me how to pray and get on my knees and seek Your face. That was what he left me, and that was far more important than any cash I have in the bank. There are many directions we can choose to travel but let's choose His way. The ONLY way!

The Bible Tells us:

Isaiah 2:5
"let us walk in the light of the Lord."

Isaiah 30:21
"Whether you turn to the right or to the left, your ears will hear a voice behind you, saying, "This is the way; walk in it."

Isaiah 40:29-31
"He gives strength to the weary and increases the weak. Even youths grow tired and weary and young men stumble and fall; but those who hope in the Lord will renew their strength.
They will soar on wings like eagles, they will run and not grow weary, they will walk and not be faint."

Jeremiah 6:16
"ask where the good way is, and walk in it, and you will find rest for your souls."

I John 1:7
"But if we walk in the light, as he is in the light, we have fellowship with one another, and the blood of Jesus, his son, purifies us from all sin."

Chapter 4

They Prayed

Seattle and the University of Washington seemed the best of worlds to Napoleon. It was a big city but it still had a country feeling. The people were nice and they were encouraging, and the coaching staff made him feel like they really wanted him. Mark Brunell was the Husky quarterback at that time and he was from the same area as Napoleon. He had attended Santa Maria High School, and that's just up the road from Lompoc. Mark is playing in the NFL with the Jacksonville Jaguars and is a real Christian witness in his own right. Brunell was one of the reasons that Napoleon made his commitment right then to go to Washington.

He wasn't quite sure what field of study to go into at first but he had always had a feel for someday becoming an actor or a color commentator on television. With that in the back of his mind he in enrolled in the school of drama, which later would help when speaking before big crowds.

It took a little getting used to at first. Being away from home is always tough in the beginning, and the rain was something that he hadn't thought much about. As time went by he managed to handle it all - even the rain.

Getting off to a good start with a great game against the Arizona Wildcats in Seattle sort of set the tone for his first season. Playing tailback on the Don James - coached team was fun for the youngster. It was exciting as well as challenging. There was mutual respect with Coach James, and Napoleon thought that he was always treated fairly. James gave him the chance to play, and that's all he could ask for. And he delivered.

That freshman year the Huskies went to the Rose Bowl, one of two times Napoleon would make it to Pasadena during his four year stay in Seattle. He would end his career as the all-time leading rusher in U of W history moving ahead of great runners like Hugh McElhenny, Beno Bryant, Joe Steele, and Greg Lewis.

Beating Michigan in the big game and being named NCAA National Champions wasn't too bad a way to start of for a kid from Lompoc.

It was also his freshman year that he met his- bride- to be Nicole DeCuire. It wasn't one of those love - at - first - sight kind of romances, but over the years they dated off and on. Nicole was from Seattle but was attending school at Pomona College in southern California majoring in history. Here she was a Washington girl going to school in California and he was a California boy going to school in Washington. It was a miracle that they ever got together, but they both realize now that this was just another part of the plan that God had for their lives.

By his senior year they started to go together on a steady basis and were married September 3, 1996.

His arrival in Seattle to start his college career was exciting but it was also a time of wondering. He wasn't sure just how things would go. This was the first time for him to be away from Lompoc and his family and friends. In Lompoc he knew the lay of the land but this big city would take some getting used to.

He never really had time to think about the fact that here he was at the University of Washington, the big time because he was thrown right into Don James scheme of things that freshman year and had to learn by playing. He knew he had a lot to learn. But learning football always came easy to Napoleon. His wife Nicole was always amazed that when he was playing with the Oakland Raiders he never seemed to bring his playbook home. He just had the instinct to pick football things up quickly. He didn't even red shirt his first year as do most freshmen at big schools.

Getting thrown into the fire gave him the opportunity to play, and he actually played a lot. Along with playing tailback he also ran kickoffs.

It was a strange feeling for the first few days when he would go out to practice and see all of these wide bodies everywhere. In high school you might see some big guys but not like these and not as many. But after a few days he found that his speed and quickness would carry him through, and he could make plays just like he did in high school.

Backing up tailbacks Jay Barry and Beno Bryant, he ended up as the third leading rusher for the Huskies with 307 yards on 67 carries with four touchdowns. He scored his first touchdown as a Husky against Kansas State on a three - yard run. His best game came against the Arizona Wildcats where he gained 71 yards on nine carries.

By the end of his freshman year Napoleon was hearing from his Husky teammates how they were praying for him, and he was starting to get Christian literature sent to him from people who also let him know they were praying for him.

Then one day in the summer after that first year he was back home in Lompoc. Out of the blue a man came up to him, a man that he had never seen before. The man stopped him and gave him a little gold pendant on a chain and started telling Napoleon how God was going to use his life. The man just went on and on about how God loved him and was going to use him. Napoleon thanked the man—-and that meeting would continue to come back to him as he started back for his second year in Seattle.

A GLIMPSE AT NAPOLEONS HEART:

It was evident that even back in those early times before I had made a real commitment to follow Jesus that people were praying for me and I really believe strongly in intercessory prayer; I'm a walking, talking example of just that kind of prayer.

When we want our prayers to have power it is important that we are both obedient to pray and that we pray believing that if we don't ask amiss our prayers will be answered. I believe there is one element to prayer that is key and that is when God has dealt with our motivations.

I believe that God deals with our motivation in our prayers, and we must seek God's will in our lives. When our motives are pure and we are truly seeking God's will in those things we're praying for, it releases a form of power, because we are not praying selfishly, we're praying the will of God, and that's why in Romans 8 we see that the spirit of God is sent forth to help us pray.

There are times when we don't know how to pray. The Bible says, " We know not how we aught to pray, but the Spirit of God makes intercession for us." I feel like there comes a time in our lives when our motivations and our hearts are so much into to the purpose of God that we're praying what God wants us to pray and not just praying selfishly.

Sometimes, when I'm feeling a little depressed and down, and when prayer is hard its at times like that that I feel I must worship. I try to take my eyes off myself and focus them upon the Lord and start to worship Him and to praise Him, not so much to ask Him for things but rather just to get my eyes on Him instead of myself all the time.

A lot of times the depression we are dealing with comes from selfishness. We feel that nobody loves us, no one cares about us, so we have a pity party. But instead of doing all that, let's get our eyes on God and He'll show us how much He loves us.

Sometimes we wonder if God hears our prayers or always answers our prayers, and I think it's important to realize what our motivation is when we pray. I think God does always answer our prayers. It may be yes, it may be no, or it may be not now. It is so important that we pray the will of God because He knows that sometimes if He answered our prayers like we think they should be answered it could destroy us. Our hearts must be ready to receive what He gives us.

I think we must be trying to live an upright life before God will answer our prayers on a consistent basis. St. John 9:31 tells us, "We know that God does not hear sinners, but if anyone is God fearing and does His will He hears him." That does not mean that God will not hear the prayer of a repentant sinner—— it doesn't mean that. The Bible says, "whosoever will may come."

When we are walking in the will of God, though, and living an upright and holy life, it causes God to want to answer our prayers and bless us.

Like so many things in life, discipline is as important in our prayer life as it is in any other facet. A hearty discipline must be developed to get into the flow of prayer. The hardest part sometimes is when we first begin a prayer life and we're not really sure if God even hears our prayers or whether we're just talking to the ceiling. We don't feel God. We don't know if He's hearing us, but through a healthy discipline we start to allow God to renew our minds, so that we are coming away from an agreement with the flesh that wants to keep us away from prayer, and we are coming into an agreement with the Spirit who wants to take us to that place of prayer.

Get up in the morning and start your day in prayer and end your day with prayer. Then during the course of the day you'll constantly be speaking about God, talking to God. As you do this you will realize that prayer is not a ritual˙. It's just simply communicating with Jesus Christ throughout your whole day.

I challenge you to prayerfully read the book of James. It will show you that our motives are so important!

THE BIBLE TELLS US:

James 1:5
" If any of you lacks wisdom, he should ask God, who gives generously to all without finding fault, and it will be given to him. But when he asks, he must believe and not doubt, because he who doubts is like a wave of the sea, blown and tossed by the wind."

Matthew 9:29
"According to your faith it will be done unto you."

Romans 1:17
"The righteous will live by faith."

Romans 5:1
"Therefore, since we have been justified through faith we have peace with God through our Lord Jesus Christ, through whom we have gained access by faith into this grace in which we now stand."

*1. # 8 Napoleon outruns the UCLA defense
for a Husky touchdown.*

NAPOLEON KAUFMAN

1994 Heisman Trophy Candidate

America's Most Exciting All-Purpose Player

2. Napoleon was a candidate for the 1994 Hesiman Trophy given to the most outstanding college player in the country.

3. Not one of Napoleon's favorite pictures from his time at the University of Washington.

4. Nip scores in a tough loss to the San Diego Chargers.

5. It's too late for Chris Mims (94) of the Chargers as Napoleon turns the corner.

6. #26 Napoleon has a big game against the Seahawks. #12 Rich Gannon is in the background.

7. 1983 Lompoc Panther team coached by Ron Mau. (not in picture) Nip is #14 and Moose Mau is # 25. Uncle Tony White is ion the top row.

8. 1985 Rangers Back row left to right, Tony White (Nip's uncle)
Ron Mau, Jim Silsbee, asst coach, Norrrn Flint, statistion. Napoleon
is # 22 in front row Moose is #30 right behind Nip.

9. Don Willis and Nip in 1991. Willis attended Cabrillo H.S. and is currently playing in the NFL.

10. 1986 Chem Kids Senior FB Team. Nip is #5 and Moose Mau
is # 21. Coach Dana Lara is in top row wearing glasses.

11. The 1981 Lions . Nip is # 25 and Moose is # 12. Ron Mau was again Napoleon's head coach..

12. 1991 after High School graduation at the Village Country Club for lunch. Left to right. Mark Owens, Barbara Mau (Ron's wife and Saint) Ron Mau, Nip and Moose Mau.

13. Lunch at the Country Club after HS graduation.

14. Awards given to the 1991 Lompoc HS football team. Nip is in front row. Some of the other players are Brian Silsbee, Bobby Singer, Paul Coffman, Degirgio and Moose Mau.

Chapter 5

He's Staying

Going back to Washington after a summer in Lompoc was something Napoleon was looking forward to. The hope of another championship year and proving to himself and everyone else that he could play big time football was a good feeling. It seemed like everything in his football life was going great. It was great coming off the year he had. But at this time his non-football life was beginning to trouble him. All through his sophomore and junior years, football was great, but he was still out there running around, partying and having what he thought at the time was a lot of fun.

His second year there would be a new head coach replacing Don James, the dean of coaches in the Pac Ten Conference. Napoleon had liked playing for James and would always be appreciative of the chance he gave him to play right from the beginning.

But Jim Lambright who replaced James was a real Kaufman supporter. One of the first things he did was hire Bill Diedrick as offensive coordinator and made it clear he wanted him to come up with something to confound the oppositions defenses that were keying on Napoleon. One thing that Diedrick did was to show Napoleon in many different positions in the backfield. Sometimes he would line up at tailback in the power I formation. Other times at split back. Again other times he would line up at wide receiver. Throw in kick off and punt returns and you better know where number 8 was or you'll get burned.

Another move that happened after Napoleon's freshman year was that Al Lavan was brought in as running backs coach and he and Napoleon hit it off from the beginning. Lavan had held that same job with the Dallas Cowboys for eight seasons and coached the legendary Tony Dorsett. According to a report in the *Los* Angeles *Times* in a column by Jim Hodges a Times writer, Hodges reports the first time Lavan saw Napoleon run for a touchdown he said, "Wow, that looks like Tony Dorsett."

Many coaches will go through a long career and never have the opportunity to work with a great running back and here Lavan has the opportunity to work with two of the best.

Napoleon was used to hearing himself compared to Dorsett and Eric Metcalf. Kaufman said, "He was a small guy, a tough guy. I like being compared to him and Eric Metcalf."

Lavan went on to say in the Hodges column, "Both are extremely quick and fast," he says. "Dorsett had great vision and acceleration, and ran with the ability to keep his pads down and make it very difficult to get a clean hit on him."

"Napoleon has the same speed," Lavan says. "Tony was a little larger in pro football, but in college they were about the same size. Dorsett was 5'11" and 185 pounds as a pro whereas Kaufman is 5'9 and 175."

"They both have great vision. They see the guy in front of them and they see five yards downfield. Lots of guys see things but can't react to them. Guys like Tony and Napoleon can react!"

"Napoleon is stronger than Tony. They both attack the defense. Kaufman has lateral movement. He can juke you, but he would rather go after you and give you just an edge to hit. That's unusual. Most small guys would rather run away from you."

There was a mutual friendship between coach and player. Napoleon found Lavan to be another father figure like his Uncle Tony, Ron Mau, and Dick Barrett had been in his earlier years. "Coach Lavan taught me a lot. Not only about football but how to have an appreciation for the game. I did a lot of growing up under his guidance." Napoleon said.

There was a lot of talk about Napoleon foregoing his last year at Washington to opt for the NFL draft but in the end he had many good reasons to stay. The headline in the *Bellevue Journal America read* **Huskies' star: I'm staying**

Yes, he was taking a chance of a career ending injury, and on any given hit a knee could be blown out and that would be the end of the story.

He was quoted in the *Bellevue Journal America* in Theresa Smith's story, "Someday I want to live in Seattle and to become involved in the community." He had enrolled three years earlier as an at risk student but will graduate in the fall of 1995 with a degree in drama. "By staying in school I want to become an example, not a stereotype."

There was a lot of pressure on the future Husky rushing champion. " The easy way would have been to declare myself for the draft," Kaufman said, "I have no doubt I can play in the National Football League. And my opportunity will come. But one thing my mom told me is that nothing in life comes easy."

Dick Barrett, his high school coach likes to say that the hardship rule was invented for players such as Napoleon who have struggled all their lives to make ends meet. But Napoleon had learned that sometimes the best way was the toughest.

Al Lavan was one of those who was happy to see Napoleon stay on as a Husky not just because it would make his job easier rather because he felt like this was a wise decision. "All of the factors were there for him to go,' Lavan said. "He certainly could have taken the money and run and there certainly was lots of money. But the more we talked about it the more I realized that other things were very important to him. It came down to him wanting to be here." Jim Lambright, UofW head coach was also thrilled to say the least.

"God willing, the money is still going to be there," said Napoleon. "Growing up not having much, people would probably expect me to go to the NFL, but this is a decision I thought about night in and night out."

Napoleon had always been a loyal person, loyal in his friendships, loyal to his family, loyal to teammates and loyal to his coaches. His final word on that story about says it all. "I'm part of this team," he said. "And that's why I'll be a Husky next year and forever."

That decision like so many in his young life would later be shown to be God ordained. Sometimes confidence is a very good thing but it doesn't replace faith. Napoleon didn't know back then what lay ahead for him but it was a time of having faith.

A Glimpse at Napoleon's Heart:

I've been asked what is faith and what's it all about and that is a little tough. I think faith is the ability for us to see God who is unseen, not seeing God with our actual eyes but with the eyes of our heart. It's when God becomes a complete reality to us even though we haven't seen Him. When I think of the word faith I think of seeing God with the eyes of our heart and that causes us to do things that we might not normally do.

When you read the scriptures and you see, especially Galatians 2: 20 the Bible says, "For I am crucified with Christ but never the less I live, yet not I but Christ lives within me, now the life I live I live by the FAITH of the Son of God." There's a time and a place in our life when God grants to us a measure of faith to believe in Him, to trust in Him and even the Bible says that we receive faith by measures from God. Then there comes a place and a time in our life when Jesus Christ has been born inside of us. He begins to rise up inside of us His faith begins to overtake our faith and then we are living by the faith of the Son of God who love us and gave his self for us.

I believe that for us to obtain that kind of faith is just a matter of us studying the scriptures and seeking God's face and then by nature what ends up happening to us is His faith begins to override our faith and the things we used to not believe God for, now by trusting Him these things we ask for become realities.

When we start seeing things happen, prayers answered, and you say, "hey what happened here?" Well, I've tapped into a dimension where God's faith has over come my faith and now I'm riding on Him and not on myself any longer. And I believe that's what Jesus wants to bring to the saints of God. We have to remember that Jesus is alive inside of us!

There comes a time in everyone's life, I'm speaking to Christians here, when our faith seems to wane, or seems almost not there. Just like we grow in every other aspects of our lives in regards to yielding to Christ, allowing Christ to lead us our faith grows over time and through tests and with situations, its God who puts us through these trials, He has the responsibility to bring me to that place I'm supposed to be at and I have the responsibility to yield to His process in an obedient fashion so He can complete these processes in my life.

Obviously there are times in our lives when we don't have the faith that we want. Think of it like this, "I have more faith now than I had two years ago," but through God's process I have learned to seek God more, so I see God more and I've learned to trust Him more and as a result of that, what God has dealt in my heart I'm beginning to mature in that area of faith that God is bringing forth by the way of Christ in my life.

We have to remember He is the potter and we are the clay. He will work in every area of our lives if we will just let Him. He wants to do a good work in us.

In Hebrews 11:24-27 it says "By faith when Moses had grown up he refused to be called the son of Pharaohs daughter choosing rather to endure ill treatment with the people of God rather than to enjoy the pleasures of sin. Considering the reproach of Christ greater riches than the treasures of Egypt for he was looking to the reward," BUT WATCH THIS "by FAITH he left Egypt not fearing the wrath of the king but he endured as seeing Him who is unseen." Amen!

God became a reality to Moses, and as he saw God with the yes of his heart God was so real it caused him to say "I'm forsaking all for I have seen Him."

THE BIBLE TELLS US:

Matthew 9:29
"According to your faith it will be done unto you."

Romans 1:17
"The righteous shall live by faith."

2 Corinthians 5:7
"We live by faith, not by sight."

Chapter 6

They're Still Praying

Napoleon's senior year was to be the big one. They had a great team coming back, and there was hype about him being a top contender for the Heisman Trophy (given to the outstanding college football player of the year). The UW sports information office kept busy throughout the summer sending out thousand of postcards showing his stats to newspapers and magazines all over the country.

Going into the start of the year the Rocky Mountain News Poll had Napoleon fifth behind tailbacks Rashaan Salaam of Colorado, Ki-Jana Carter of Penn. State, and quarterbacks, Kerry Collins from Penn. State and Alcorn State's Steve McNair. But there was one fan that thought differently, his high school coach Dick Barrett. "I'm real prejudiced, but I think he's the best player in the country," Barrett said. " No other tailback is being defended with eight and nine man fronts."

And then one night things caught up with him. He was out at a club with some friends, actually he stepped outside the club for a few minutes. When he headed back inside the club the club bouncer wouldn't let him back in. Things got out of hand and a fight broke out. A friend of Napoleon's grabbed him and a friend of the bouncer grabbed the bouncer, but while Napoleon's friend was holding him the bouncers' friend let him go and he punched Napoleon in the face. The bouncer really threw a punch.

Napoleon's eye sank down into his face. Here he was about to start the most important football season yet and he couldn't see straight. Though surgery was required, in God's graciousness the eye responded to treatment, and by the time the season started he was okay.

We might think that an incident like that, a nearly career ending incident, would have gotten his attention but all it did was slow him down a little. He was still out there drinking and partying. But something was different. He would tell his teammates that he thought that God was trying to tell him something. He felt a kind of tug. "This is God," he would say to himself. At that time he couldn't grasp the fact that God was dealing with him.

As his senior year went by he was still playing great football. He ended up becoming the schools all-time career leader in rushing with 4,041 yards and 5,658 in all-purpose yards. He set a single season standard for Husky running backs with 1,390 yards by rushing for over 1000 yard per season for three years in a row. This feat had only been accomplished by four other Pac 10 Conference running backs and none of the from the UW.

When asked about what he thought about the season, "It's been great. I'm very happy with my season. I improved as a player in every aspect of the game. I just wished we could have won a few more games."

Many pro teams were expressing an interest in obtaining his services. By finishing out his four years as a Husky, Napoleon gave himself a chance to move up in the NFL draft. A draft expert and editor of the Pro Football Weekly said at the time, " He was a fourth round pick and now he's a second round pick. I thought he was spectacular at times. He's too gifted a runner not to play in the league, (NFL) but exactly how he'll fit into a team is tough to say."

Napoleon thought that the Dallas Cowboys and the New England Patriots had expressed the most interest but it was a wait - and – see time. The NFL draft didn't happen until mid April.

He was chosen to play in two post- season senior games, the East-West Shrine game and the Senior Bowl. He toned things down in his non-football world to concentrate on becoming a professional football player for by whichever team drafted him.

NAPOLEON'S CAREER STATS AT THE UNIVERSITY OF WASHINGTON:

Rushing:

Year	G-S	TC	Yds	Lost	Net	Avg.	Td	LG
1991	11-0	67	331	24	307	4.6	4	19
1992	11-6	162	1087	42	1045	6.5	6	70
1993	11-11	226	1357	58	1299	5.7	14	58t
1994	11-11	235	1405	81	1390	5.5	9	91t
Totals	44-28	710	4232	206	4041	5.7	33	91t

Receiving:

Year	G-S	Rec.	Yds	Avg.	TD	LG
1991	11-0	5	39	7.8	0	17
1992	11-6	13	47	3.6	0	21
1993	11-11	23	139	6.0	0	27
1994	11-11	24	199	8.3	0	41
Totals	44-28	65	424	6.5	0	41

All Purpose Yards:

Year	G	Rush	Rec	Punt	KO	Total	Avg.
1991	11	307	39	66	119	531	48.3
1992	11	1045	47	269	89	1450	131.8
1993	11	1299	139	25	388	1851	168.3
1994	11	1390	199	8	229	1826	166.0
Totals	44	4041	424	368	825	5654	128.5

Punt Returns:

Year	G	Punt	Yards	Avg.	Td	Long
1991	11	8	66	8.3	0	16
1992	11	19	269	14.2	0	65
1993	11	4	25	6.3	0	14
1994	11	3	8	2.7	0	12
Totals	44	34	368	10.8	0	65

Kick Off Returns:

Year	G	KO	Yards	Avg.	TD	Long
1991	11	7	119	17.0	0	25
1992	11	5	89	17.8	0	25
1993	11	15	388	25.9	0	50
1994	11	9	229	25.4	0	34
Totals	44	36	825	22.9	0	50

And his prayer was answered. He was drafted in the first round, the 18th player, taken, by the Oakland Raiders, his favorite team. It was a dream come true. The California boy had been picked by a California team. (Actually he was drafted by the then Los Angeles Raiders, but he didn't play a game in L.A. as the team moved back to Oakland for his rookie season,)

Not only was everything going well on the football front but it seemed that every aspect of his life was picture perfect. He bought a house in Seattle right across from Lake Washington. He bought his mother a house in Lompoc. He had a Mercedes, a Cadillac, and a truck. He had all this stuff, but yet he would sit in the big house wondering . . .what's it all about? Later when he looked back on things he would recall Solomon's words, "Vanity, vanity, all is vanity." It was certain that material things weren't making him happy, because he had about all the material things you could ask for. No, there was something down deep inside that was tugging on him. That feeling he had had since he was eleven years old and was baptized at the little Baptist church.

All those years God was working on him. He later learned that people had been praying for him, and he remembered how he had heard other people had prayed for this one or that one for fifteen or twenty years and then, all of a sudden, that person comes to Christ

A GLIMPSE AT NAPOLEON'S HEART:

I'm sure glad that all those people that were praying for me all those years didn't give up on me. I bet there were times when they thought their prayers would never be answered.

We all should take the word "quit" out of our vocabulary. There is just no place for that word in our lives. If ever a four letter word was a dirty word it's "quit." Sometimes it looks like the easiest course to take but in the long run it will be disastrous.

The Lord lets us know about how powerful intercessory prayer can be in both telling us how to use it and He himself used it when he prayed for all of us.

What this tells me is that we must keep on keepen' on until the Lord comes again. If you have needs in your life, if you need a physical touch in your body, if you have an unsaved loved one, or if you just need a time of rest, bring it to Jesus. He's the only one who can truly meet your needs or the needs of a loved one.

He may use other people to bring things about. He may bring you to a good doctor who can treat your physical body. He may bring a new job that you need through another brother in Christ. He may send someone to minister to that unsaved loved one. He may even put you in a sick bed to get your attention so you can get that much- needed rest.

Never give up! Never stop praying for that lost soul that God has put on your heart. It will be neat when we get to heaven and we run into someone that we're praying for and didn't know the out come of that persons life until that moment——wow, what a day that will be. Praise God. And we all have people that we are, or should be praying for. It is so important that we approach our prayer life with boldness knowing that God has promised to honor our requests if we pray according to His will. What could be more in God's will than our loved ones be saved? Nothing! That is the reason that God sent His only Son so that lost souls could be saved.

But, most of all, when you hear the call from God on your life, when you feel that tugging that you know can't come from anyone else but the Savior, heed that call, and don't put it off. Jesus said, "If I be lifted up I will draw all men to Me." It's the Master who calls us. All we have to do is obey . . . trust and obey.

It is so easy to put off that call. It never seems to come at the right time. We've always got this or that to do, and then we'll come. But Jesus tells us, "Let the dead bury the dead." What He means is that you can always find a reason, an excuse to not follow Him. Everyday, every hour you put it off is one more day or one more hour that you have not spent with the One that loves you the most.

There is nothing in this world that can compare with eternity with the Creator of the Universe, God Almighty. Can you imagine the patience that God must have to put up with our procrastination?

Heed that tug! Hear that plea! Now is the time for salvation!

THE BIBLE TELLS US:

John 17:9
"I pray for them . . ."

Ephesians 6:18
"And pray in the Spirit on all occasions with all kinds of prayers and requests. With this in mind, be alert and always keep on praying for all the saints."

1 Chronicles 5:20
". . . He answered their prayers because they trusted Him."

Mark 11:24
"Therefore I tell you, whatever you ask for in prayer; believe that you have received it, and it will be yours."

Psalm 27:4
"One thing I ask of the Lord, this is what I seek: that I might dwell in the house of the Lord all the days of my life."

Psalm 62:1-2
"My soul finds rest in God alone; my salivation comes from Him. He alone is my rock and my salivation; He is my fortress, I will never be shaken."

Psalm 6:9
"The Lord has heard my cry for mercy; the Lord accepts my prayer."

Chapter 7

Professional Football

On April 23, 1995 the bay area newspaper headlines read like this:

Raiders pick Kaufman, ignore Heisman—winner— Raiders Score Well in NFL Draft—RAIDERS: Pick Kaufman—Kaufman No. 1 on Davis' Short List of Backs— Raiders option to draft Kaufman with 18th pick.

Ever since Napoleon had known what the NFL draft was he wanted to be part of it. That was his goal from the time he played for Ron Mau in the Pop Warner leagues. Professional football! That was the pinnacle, the National Football League, that was where only the best earned the right to play.

On draft day he was quoted in Mike Taylor's column as saying, "I can't explain how excited I am. Being from California and growing up watching the Raiders every weekend. This definitely means a lot to me, and hey I'm ready to play. This is great! The Raiders are a perfect situation for me."

The 1995 draft was one of the best in a long while for the NFL. Players like Ki Jana Carter of Penn Sate, Steve McNair Alcorn State, Kerry Collins Penn State, Joey Galloway from Ohio State, J.J. Stokes of UCLA, Derek Alexander, Florida State, Warren Sapp, Miami, Tyrone Wheatly from Michigan, James Stewart of Tennessee, and a number of others who would go on to have outstanding careers in pro football ball.

Napoleon's class coming into the NFL was a good one and now it was time to play where the best play. Great backs like Gayle Sayers, Jim Brown, Emmett Smith, Barry Sanders, Marcus Allen and the list goes on, all played in the premier league and now it was Napoleons turn.

In high school he had to prove he wasn't too small. And at the University of Washington he had to constantly prove that he was not too small to play major college football and he did just that by setting all kinds of Husky records along the way. For a guy who was supposed to be too small he never missed a game in four years at Seattle!

But it was about to start all over again. Being taken in the first round, the 18th player taken over all would about say it all but there was one doubter, Raider head coach Mike White. White wasn't convinced that Napoleon could be an every down back, he said that "he probably should be used for kick off returns, spot plays and third downs."

Staying in character Napoleon just said, " That's fine with me. I've returned kicks for four years. I did a fine job at the college level, and I'm prepared to come in and excel at the next level." But that wasn't where Napoleon wanted things to stay. He knew he could be an outstanding everyday running back. He didn't feel he was a small back, just a short one. And to his way of thinking with his strength, his size was actually a plus for him. "It's hard to hit what you can't see!"

His Rookie year of 1995 saw Napoleon see action in all sixteen games as a reserve running back. He also performed well as a kick off return specialist breaking an 84 – yard run for a touchdown against the Indianapolis Colts.

His stats were not the kind of numbers that he was used to posting but they certainly were very respectable. He rushed for 490 yards on 108 carries for a team high average of 4.5 yards per carry. He returned 22 kick offs for an additional 572 yards.

His first regular season game in the NFL saw him gain 32 yards on five carries, one a 16 yard touchdown scamper against the San Diego Chargers. This was just the start. He would be ready when his time came.

Napoleon started making believers out of most of the doubters in 1996 but Coach White was still concerned about his being durable enough. He not only was durable enough but he played in all sixteen games and started nine at running back for the Silver and Black.

His 5.8 yards per carry led the NFL and he was ranked in the top ten in rushing in the AFC. He was the Raiders leading rusher with 874 yards on 150 carries. Getting 548 yards on 25 kickoff returns was a team high at 21.9 yards per return. He ran for 100 yards or more three times.

It was Napoleon's belief in himself, and his work ethic that he brought to the Raider facility every day, along with an attitude of can do, that fueled his improvement each season. He is a firm believer in having a good attitude!

A Glimpse at Napoleon's Heart:

An attitude in many ways is our prospective- basically what we see. A lot of times our attitude is reflective of how we see things. God takes our lives and ... most of the times we have a negative attitude that comes from a negative perspective on a situation.

We catch ourselves looking at everything in a rigid manner. People are always upset because their perspective on life comes from negativity, and that is reflected in everything they do. Everything is negative because their perspective on life is negative.

But then God opens your eyes and causes you to see things from a positive perspective. It's like when God told Ezekiel to look at that valley of dry bones. If he had gone by his own perspective it would have caused a great deal of negativity to rise up in his heart.. He could have thought those bones were dry, they looked like nothing. They're dead, but when you've gotten close to God and are starting to get His prospective then that changes your prospective. Now you can see those dry bones beginning to come to life!

So we begin looking at things in a positive manner, and we deny what's bad, and we see hope whereas before, at least in my life, I never saw hope. But Jesus says not to be afraid when we see the negative things, it's just a sign of the times. When the rest of the world is going crazy you have God's attitude so you can see things in a positive light, and you don't have to be afraid.

When things look all messed up and you get close to God he opens your eyes so you can clearly see the whole picture and that's what changes your attitude. Its like fourth down and one, everyone's upset, they're saying what are we going to do, what'll happen if we don't get this first down? But when you're walking with God, and he gives you that confidence, that boldness to see that its only one little yard and we've got the first down. How we look at that yard is so important. If it looks like a mile to you, an impossible task, try looking at that yard through God's eyes and it will look like a sure thing to you.

Remember, you play a part in this whole attitude thing. You have a choice. It was that way with Ezekiel. He had a choice to make when he looked at those dry bones. Was he going to look at these bones and judge their condition from what he saw, or was he going to look at those bones and judge them by what God says about them?

We can go with what the flesh is saying or we can see what God is saying. What does God's word say concerning my situation? When I understand His thinking, then my attitude begins to change. I take God at His word and believe His promises. There is always that choice to make – His way or my way. I choose His way of thinking!

Having a bad attitude can destroy you! All the hopelessness, the down feelings, all that stuff begins to accumulate in your life and weigh you down, and you begin to feel heavy. That's when you tend to blame everything on everybody else. But its not them, its just your prospective, its your attitude.

The way to get rid of a bad attitude is to first acknowledge that you have one. Go to God and say, "God, I've got a bad attitude." Then repent, turn away from that and seek God's tender mercy. Allow Him through His word to show you where you may have faltered and gotten off track and allow Him by His word to really change you, change your heart.

Obedience goes hand in hand with having a good attitude. Obedience is a total denial of your will. I believe you get to a place where you give up your will in exchange for God. That is something that all of us struggle with. Before we met God we were so used to running our own lives. We have to come into submission to God.

Remember when Jesus told His disciples to go to a certain place and find a colt tied up and they were to bring it to Jesus for Him to ride into Jerusalem. Now that colt had never been ridden, but all Jesus did was touch the colt and his will was broken, and it came into submission to the Lord. Then He got on and rode the colt through town. What God is looking for is that same breaking in our lives when He touches us and we give up our will.

That was the whole issue of Adam and Eve in the garden. God had given them free will to choose right or wrong. He needed something to try the relationship and to see if they were willing to obey or not. And very clearly they showed they had that free will to obey or disobey.

Many think that delayed obedience is as bad as no obedience, but I think Jesus addressed that issue when he was speaking to the Pharisees - when he spoke about a man who said he was going to obey, but went on to disobey.

There are times when we do struggle. It's like Jonah who delayed obedience to God in going to Nineveh to preach repentance. It took a near ship-wreck, a swim in the deep, and being swallowed by a fish before he decided to obey God.

There are going to be times when we are pulled and are not sure what is right or wrong, when that happens to me, I do nothing. I wait until I believe God is giving me the word to advance.

THE BIBLE TELLS US:

Philippians 2: 5-11

Your attitude should be the same as that of Christ Jesus. Who, being in very nature God, did not consider equality with God something to be grasped, but made himself nothing, taking the very nature of a servant, being made in human likeness.

And being found in appearance as a man, he humbled himself and became obedient to death—-even death on a cross!

Therefore God exalted him to the highest place and gave him the name that is above every name, that at the name of Jesus every knee should bow, in heaven and on earth and under earth, and every tongue confess that Jesus Christ is Lord, to the glory of God the father.

Ephesians 4:22-24

You were taught, with regard to your former way of life, to put off your old self, which is being corrupted by its deceitful desires; <u>to be made new in the attitude of your minds.</u>

Hebrews 4: 12-13

For the word of God is living and active. Sharper than any double-edged sword, it penetrates even dividing soul and spirit, joints and marrow; it judges the thoughts and attitudes of the heart.

15. 1991 CIF Championship game. Lompoc 12 Arroyo Grande 6. Ron Mau is next to Nip and Paul Coffman is # 50.

*16. Nip receiving High School award in 1991. Coach Dick Barrett
in background.*

17. Nip and Mark Owens at the Mau's house in 1991. Both Napoleon and Mark stayed with the Mau's for their senior year.

*18. Moose Mau, Napoleon and Mark Owens
at the Mau's house in 1991.*

19. Hangin' with buds in 1991. Paul Coffman, Moose, Scott Morgan, Nip, and Mark Owens.(Morgan is currently playing baseball with the Angels)

20. 1991 Nip, Moose and Mark Owens are oiling down Mrs. Mau's cupboards.

21. The Kaufman's celebrate birthdays.

22. Nicole and little Nathaniel at about six months.

23. "Little Nip" says he's a Warrior too.

24. It's Christmas time at the Kaufman house.

25. Nathaniel says, "he's not heavy he's my brother
(Napoleon IV on top)

26. Napoleon and his boys.

27. "Little Nip gives brother Nathaniel a big hug!

28. Its Captain Nip and Little brother on the keyboards.

29. Napoleon IV belts out a song.

30. Nathaniel sings too!

31. Nip and Little Nip take in the action at the game.

Chapter 8

The Tug

Now here it was late June in 1996, a bright sunny day with the temperature a smoldering 102 degrees, and Napoleon' s was driving his shiny new Ford Explorer through the winding roads of the wine country, heading to the Oakland Raiders summer training camp in Napa, California. Those hot days and cool nights were what gives the grapes the sweetness that California is famous for, and that stifling heat that suppressed some activity was also just the ticket for getting professional football players into shape. It was time to start a second year in professional football with the Raiders of the NFL, and he was ready.

To look at Napoleon Kaufman's life you would think, "Man he's got it made!" He's playing good football with the team he always wanted to play with. He had a new house, cars, money in the bank and a beautiful fiancé. But in his heart there was an emptiness. It was that tugging. It was still there, and it was getting stronger. He knew that a vague discontentment with his own accomplishments, financial gains, morality, and other areas of his life. He could see that God drawing and calling him. But like so many people he continued to put it off.

A couple of days later at camp he was out on the football field cussing and talking smack with the guys when a Christian brother, a teammate by the name of Jerone Davison looked at him and said, "Hey man, you don' t even look like the type of guy that should be out here cussing and acting crazy like the rest of these brothers. Don't you know God can use your life?"

There it was again. "God can use your life!" Ever since he had arrived at the University of Washington to play college football some five years earlier people had been telling him that they were praying for him and they had been sending him Christian literature. But when Jerone said that to him, it really challenged his identity for the first time. All of his life he had been living to please other people, trying to appear a certain way, because he knew it would be pleasing to everybody else. But that wasn' t who he really was. He was putting on a great show, a façade to please people. In his heart he knew he wasn't being real. He was portraying something other than the real Napoleon Kaufman.

When he first heard Jerone say those words, he felt he had to justify his actions. "Man, I gotta be out here cussing and stuff. I' ve got to show these brothers I'm tough." He knew in his heart that was foolish and he was tired of doing it.

Back in his training camp room at the hotel all he could hear was that wee small voice inside him saying, "Don't you know God can use you? Don' t you know Jesus loves you and has a wonderful plan for your life? He is genuine and real and He wants you to be genuine and real too!"

Right there in that hotel room on August 28, 1996 on that hot summer afternoon Napoleon Kaufman got really honest with himself and with the Lord, and at last he asked the Lord Jesus to come into his heart and be his Savior and Lord. He asked Jesus to forgive him for all the things he had done wrong. It was a new beginning. It was the Lords wooing, and He was successful as always. Napoleon Kaufman was born again! Born of the Spirit of God! Not a physical birth, not just the climax of a period of gestation; it was the beginning of a new life and a new relationship with God the Creator. Ephesians 2:18 says: " For through him we both have access to the Father by one Spirit." The old emptiness and longing to be real and clean were gone. Praise God!

And that was just the beginning!

Immediately he started reading the scriptures. He couldn't get enough of God's wonderful Word. It was awesome how the Holy Spirit had given him that hunger and thirst for the Bible. It was new and exciting, and so fulfilling, so satisfying. Every word seemed to come alive to him. It was now personal. Napoleon knew this was his reason for living. This was why he was born to know God and be known by Him, and to make Him known to others.

He wanted to shout it from the rooftops. He was telling everyone who would hold still long enough to hear what the Lord had done for him. This was not something he felt he was supposed to do or had to do, it was a great privilege, a joy bubbling up inside of him, really good news!

There was real purpose and meaning to life after that. He was free to be all God wanted him to be. He now was genuine, clean, and in right relationship with God and his fellowman. Jesus said, "Come and you will see." (John 1:39) Napoleon could see! Yes, his eyes had been opened spiritually to see the truth. "And I will ask the Father and He will give you another Counselor to be with you forever—-the Spirit of Truth." John 14:17

He couldn't wait to get to Jerone Davison to tell him what had happened to him. But the amazing thing was that Jerone was less than enthusiastic at first, and he needed some persuading that Napoleon wasn't just kidding

"No Jerone, really I'm not kidding about something as serious as this, I'm giving my life to God. I'm really giving my life to God. You'll see man. It's real! Everything is going to be different from now on. I've accepted the Lord."

Soon after that, training camp broke and he went back home and told his longtime girlfriend Nicole DeCuire, who was soon to be his wife. (The Lord was faithful to show him that was a top priority.) "Sit down here honey, I've got to tell you something . . . Nicole, I gave my life to Jesus."

Nicole was shocked at first to say the least. She wondered how this was going to change him and their relationship and their lives. And sure enough, it all changed for the better. She had been raised a Catholic, had even attended parochial schools growing up. At first Nicole thought he had gone off the deep end, but in a short time, with the positive changes that were evident in Napoleon, with God's word and the deep love and commitment he had, it was a natural response for her to want that intimate relationship with the Lord for herself, and she too asked the Lord Jesus to be her Savior.

Napoleon started studying God's word six or seven hours a night. He was totally caught up. He couldn't get enough of it. He would go to practice and talk to Jerone. He'd chase him all around the football field asking him questions about things he had read in the Bible. Some of the other Raider players came to Jerome and said, "Jerome, you've got to talk to Napoleon, he's taking this thing too far."

Napoleon didn't care. At last he knew that God could use him, and he was excited at the prospect of just how he might be used. Just being used by God almighty was awesome!

It was true to him that;

"The gospel came to you not simply with words, but also with power."

I Thessalonians 1:5

Chapter 9

The Big Year

Many things happened to Napoleon in 1997 both on and off the football field. Exciting, happy and rewarding things that made his life easier. One major factor was Joe Bugel replaced Mike White as head coach and his idea of how to best utilize his speedster running back was quit a bit different than his predecessor. Bugel would get the ball into Napoleon's hands one - way or the other.

Before the Denver game Bugel announced his game plan. "Play some defense and give the ball to Napoleon Kaufman." Remarking on his coach's declaration Napoleon said, "You should have seen the look in those Denver defensive players eyes. It was like they were the dogs and I had a pork chop tied around my neck."

Now that he was the Raider fans darling it was just natural that the fans had to bestow a nickname on their hero. The San Jose Mercury News ran a contest and here are the six finalists and Napoleons thoughts on them;

The Conqueror – "That has a nice ring to it."
The Running Man – "Its simple, but it kind of says it all."
Bullet – "I've thought of that one before.
    It sounds pretty good."
Mighty Mite – "Harvey Williams calls me that."
Turbo – "It just sounds fast."

Nipster – "Some guys call me that anyway, so it feels natural."

On the football field he began where he left off the year before, again leading the Raiders in rushing with 1294 yards, second highest single season total in Oakland history on 272 carries. He added an additional 403 yards receiving, placing him sixth best in total yards from scrimmage with 1697 yards in the NFL.

His 4.8 yards per carry tied for best in the AFC among running backs. He had six 100 - yard games and scored eight touchdowns. He accounted for nine plays of 40 yards or more.

It was this season that he broke Bo Jackson's single game rushing record by going for 227 yards on 28 carries (8.7 yards per carry) against the Denver Broncos. In that same game he had a career-long run of 83 yards for a touchdown. That was the longest run in the NFL in 1997.

Napoleon had his first 100 - yard day against the Atlanta Falcons in Atlanta (9/14) running for 140 yards on 14 carries and two touchdowns. One of those touchdowns came on a game-high 61- yard burst past four would be tacklers.

The Top Raider Rushing Games in History
(SF Chronicle 10/27/97)
1. **Napoleon Kaufman 227 yards Oct 18, 1997 vs Denver**
2. Bo Jackson 220 yards Nov 20, 1987 vs Seattle
3. Clem Daniels 187 yards Oct 20, 1963 vs Jets
4. Clem Daniels 187 yards Dec 9, 1962 at Houston
5. Hewritt Dixon 187 yards Sept 29, 1968 at Houston
6. Marcus Allen 173 yards Nov 25, 1964 vs Broncos

Everything on the football field was going about as well as it could but what was happening off the field was even more exciting to Napoleon. Being ordained to preach found him traveling all over to spread the gospel. This was what he was born to do.

He was getting into the Word and the Word was getting

into him. The tug was starting to get stronger and when he about thought God was calling him to the full time ministry God would have to say, "Not now. Not quit yet." Napoleon was now the chaplain for the Raiders and enjoyed the fellowship with his teammates.

It was good that God had planted him on a team that had such strong Christians. Men like Steve Wisniewski, Darrell Ashmore, Tim Combs and a host of other believers.

Becoming a father for the second time when little Nathanael was born just added to the wonderful life that was becoming his. "Little Nip" now the nickname bestowed on Napoleon IV was keeping his dad in shape trying to keep up with him.

Being involved in the community and helping other people was something that seemed to come natural Napoleon starting while he was at the University of Washington in Seattle. He was on the Board of Directors of the Boys and Girls Club, one of his pet projects.

Monte Poole, sports writer with *The Oakland Tribune* has written many nice things about Napoleon during the years that he has been with the Raiders but one of his finest tributes was the following; *"Napoleon Kaufman, like most of society, sees them at intersections all over the Bay Area, men and women and children with mouths that beg, eyes that plead and signs that serve as their last, desperate grasp at dignity.*

Signs like:" Will work for food."

Kaufman, like most of society, sees these people from the comfort of his own vehicle. For the Oakland Raiders star running back, that little German luxury car is synonymous with the highest level of success.

But unlike most of society, Kaufman doesn't stroke his conscience with a mere sigh of helplessness, or limit his assistance to one sad eyed glimpse through a tinted window.

He actually sets out to do something. He offers a hand. A bit of inspiration. A slice of his most precious commodity.

Time!

"I drive down High Street and see people carrying those signs,"

Kaufman said. *"A lot of people will feel sorry for them, but they don't want to do anything to help. It's easy to drive by and see people in a bad situation, but it won't get any better if you don't help."*

Kaufman is one of six Bay Area athletes who will be honored for their contributions to the community. He wants to reach people on the fringe. At risk youth. The disadvantaged. Those that feel trapped in the worse kind of cycle.

"To let people know there is a way out, that they can make it." He said. "People get caught up in believing there's no hope. Showing them hope is my job."

Kaufman, an ordained minister, routinely visits local schools, churches and youth centers. He delivered the keynote address at a recent symposium at Laney College. He taped a "Jeopardy" segment to benefit the American Red Cross and spoke at Oakland Tech High in support of the Youth of Valor Awards.

He conducted his Christian Football Camp in his hometown of Lompoc, raising $5,000. to aid college students.

"I feel good about that because I know how hard it was for me when I went off to college," he said. "I didn't have a dime in my pocket. I grew up in a single parent home and know how hard it can be for today's youth, so many of which are raised the same way."

Napoleon has known what it means to be without and now he can say he knows what it is to be well off but that time of poverty isn't long past and he still can remember how it felt to be a kid that didn't have what other kids had and the things that youngsters resort to try and level the playing field themselves. He feels that his calling to preach is all part of the Masters plan to put him in a position to really be a helper.

Sometimes we wonder why? Why does this have to happen to me? Did I really need that in my life? Why couldn't God have chosen an easier way for me? Those are questions we all ask, those of us that go through tough times, and all of us will go through tough times sometime in our lives.

Why did Napoleon have to grow up so poor? Why did he have to be raised by his mother alone when the Bible tells us how important a father is in the home? Why did he have to constantly battle with coaches, sports writers, and even fans over his size? Why, why, why?

Sure Napoleon had these questions from early on and it took him awhile to see the why of it all. No one can truly say they know the whys for all these things but they can realize that there is One who does know every why and reason for every thing that happens to us on a minute – by- minute basis.

If Napoleon had never suffered through his troubled child-hood how could he relate or much more, how could he minister to those going through horrible times now? If he had not known the wealth, fame and success that comes from being a famous sports star how could he relate to or minister to those with plenty.

NAPOLEON'S NUMBERS AS A RAIDER:

Rushing

YEAR	NO	YARDS	AVG	LG	TD
1995	108	490	4.5	28	1
1996	150	874	5.8*	77	1
1997	272	1,294	4.8	83	6
1998	217	921	4.2	80	2
1999	138	714	5.2	75	2
TOTAL	885	4,293	4.9	83	12

*Led NFL

Receiving

YEAR	NO	YARDS	AVG	LG	TD
1995	9	62	6.9	18	0
1996	22	143	6.5	19	1
1997	40	403	10.1	70	2
1998	25	191	7.6	29	0
1999	18	181	10.1	50	1
TOTAL	114	980	8.6	70	4

Kickoff Returns

YEAR	NO	YARDS	AVG	LG	TD
1995	22	572	26.0	84	1
1996	25	548	21.9	39	0
1997	0	0	0.0	0	0
1998	0	0	0.0	0	0
1999	42	831	19.8	48	0
TOTAL	89	1,951	21.9	48	1

A Glimpse at Napoleon's Heart:

My life with Jesus just gets better each day. I can't wait to get up and see what He's got in store for me. My life was and is one miracle after another. Praise God!

One of the things I like about the five- fold ministry is that it doesn't limit God in any way. Miracles, I believe happen everyday, all over and many times we don't see them but that's because we aren't looking.

Just God's daily provisions for us each day should be considered a miracle, as should so many things we take for granted. But sometimes God allows certain circumstances to come into our life so that His love and compassion may be shown.

In my life I don't know where I would be today if God had not placed me where I was as a child and then a young man. I sure didn't like the poverty and all that goes with it but looking back there was a reason that God allowed it and now I'm glad He did.

I don't know what you call a miracle if my life and what has happened to me is not a miracle. Sometimes I just shake my head when I look around today and see how God has blessed me and then think back from where I came. That's a miracle, big time!

We have to believe that Jesus is who He says He is and that he has all the power over our lives and nothing can come into our lives that He doesn't allow. Physical suffering can be a terrible thing but ask a person who has miraculously been healed by God from cancer and hear what they have to say about getting cancer in the first place. Most people will say that" if I hadn't got cancer God would not have gotten my attention and I don't know where I might have ended up but now I know I'm going to heaven to live eternally with my heavenly Father."

Look around you and see if you can see a miracle that has happened to you and you really have never given it a second thought. Maybe it's your loving spouse. He/she just didn't happen to come into your life by accident/ There are no accidents. God has the perfect spouse for you if you allow Him to pick that mate for you. That's a miracle!

How about those kids of yours? Just the whole process of conception and birth is a miracle and do we look at it that way? Probably not, but try seeing your children as little miracles from God who can be with you for all eternity.

God may even give you the opportunity to be part of someone's miracle. You may be that doctor who treats supposedly terminal patient and through your diligence to learn all you could about medicine and God's miracle working power that patient is healed and now he's out there telling everyone about the power of God because he's seen it first hand and you had a big part in that.

Maybe you are a prosperous businessman or woman who can help a young poor child get a college education. God does not give us wealth just for our own pleasures but we are to be good stewards.

Possibly you could be someone who has not had the benefit of a college education and unable to be a doctor or maybe God has chosen you to work in a way other than through your finances. But what ever it is God does have a purpose for all of us. Everyone is as important as the next to God.

THE BIBLE TELLS US:

1 Chronicles 16: 12
"Remember the wonders he has done, his miracles, and the judgments he pronounced."

Psalms 77:14
"You are the God who performs miracles; you display your power among the people."

John 14:11
"Believe me when I say that I am in the Father and the Father is in me; or at least believe on the evidence of the miracles themselves."

Romans 12: 9-16
"Love must be sincere. Hate what is evil; cling to what is good. Be devoted to one another in brotherly love. Honor one another above yourselves. Never be lacking in zeal, but keep your spiritual fervor, serving the Lord. Be joyful in hope, patient in affliction, faithful in prayer. Share with God's people who are in need. Practice hospitality.
Bless those who persecute you, bless and do not curse. Rejoice with those who rejoice; mourn with those who mourn. Live in harmony with one another. Do not be proud, but be willing to associate with people of low position. Do not be conceited."

Chapter 10

Transformed

It was now 1998, two years after Napoleon surrendered his life to God, his fourth year playing for the Raiders, when an athlete is at the peak of his career and Napoleon was feeling the call to give up professional football and go into the ministry full-time. This was not a knee jerk reaction on his part. He simply continued to follow the Lord's leading to the best of his ability as a new Christian.

For a young man who only a couple of years earlier had given his life to God to be used as God saw fit, things were starting to seem very confusing, but yet also quite clear. It seemed that each week something different or someone different was being sent into his life by God to open new doors and Napoleon continued to follow as he felt led by God.

Ever since his friend and teammate. Jerone Davison had said those words to him about God wanting to use his life, Napoleon was trying to put everything that was happening into perspective. He was most concerned that he see things from God's perspective and that he would move as God directed and in God's time.

Ironically, the year after he gave his life to Jesus he led the NFL in yards per carry, averaging 5.8 yards per carry, a Raider record. It was at that time people were already telling him that if he became a Christian he'd "loose the eye of the tiger." He would loose that aggressiveness that had always been his trade-

mark. It was not to be so. This was his best year in professional football and he had just become a Christian.

But things began to unfold that he could not have guessed
would happen just a few short years earlier.

A GLIMPSE AT NAPOLEON'S HEART:

*I was so hungry for God and His word that I couldn't get enough
of it. I was in church every chance I got. Then things started happening. It was about one year to the day that I got saved that I went
to see my friend from the Raiders, Jerone Davison receive his license
to preach. His church was the one I was attending at the time, The
Church of God in Christ. He and several other men of the church
were being ordained to preach. I said, "Hey, I'm going to enjoy this!*

*Here we were sitting in the pews with my friends being ordained
and then out of the blue Pastor James Davis called me to the pulpit.
He said, "Napoleon, I want you to stand. There's no mystery to all of
us in this church that you have a calling from God to preach His
word, so we want you to stand up and we're going to license you to
preach."*

*"I got up trembling. I couldn't believe this was happening to me.
That was in 1997 and there I was, licensed to preach! I started traveling for God as He started to open doors, and the Spirit of God started to move, and God started smiling on me. That was the year that
I rushed for 1200 yards with the Raiders. It was a great year!*

*Then 1998 came around and the Oakland Raiders hired Jon
Gruden as head coach. Jon would be the youngest coach in the
National Football League. I thought it was a good move and I liked
playing for Jon. But it was things that were happening off the football field that were getting . . . different.*

*We had gone into Denver to play the Broncos on a Monday night.
Monday night football had always been good to the Raiders but I had
hurt my ankle. I was having a tough year on the field in general, getting hurt and little nagging injuries that seemed to linger all year
long, I still started 13 games but missed three due to those ankle and
groin injuries. I led the team in rushing for the third straight year
with 921 yards with 217 carries. Like I said football was going good*

but now things were heating up off the field. God was dealing with me.

I was sitting in McDonalds in the Denver airport talking with my teammate and friend Steve Wisniewski. We'd just lost the game to Denver. I said, "You know man, I feel God's calling me to the ministry." Here I am sharing this with Steve on how I think God is calling me into full time ministry when another Raider friend, Darrell Ashmore comes up to me and says, "Hey man, there are two guys here to see you. They say they want to pray for you. One of the guys is the pastor of my cousins' church and they said they came down to pray for you."

There was a Caucasian guy and a black guy. When I walked up to them, one of them said, "I feel a word of the Lord for this young man. Come on let's pray." So Steve Wisniewski, Tim Combs another Raider, Darrell Ashmore, Darrell's friend and me, all get in this big circle right there in the middle of the Denver airport. There were people walking by wondering what in the world is going on with these guys. So here we are in the circle and we start praying and the Caucasian guy looks at me and says, "You are feeling God calling you to the ministry. God is calling you to the ministry. He's going to use you in His ministry."

He starts telling me all these things about how God was calling me and how He was going to use me. What he didn't know was that just five minutes before this I was talking to Steve at McDonalds about the very same thing.

We just took off praying in the spirit. We talked, we cried out to God right there in the airport. It just erupted. Everyone just started shouting. It was amazing. Steve, Tim, and Darrell all knew what these guys didn't know - that I had just said the same things to them.

One of the men started prophesying all of this stuff about how God was calling me. So I started to think then . . . hey maybe I need to do this now! But that wasn't to be the case.

That was in November of 1998. Right after that God took me through a whole season of repentance, a season in which God just started dealing with my heart about what it means to be a preacher of His gospel. (From the time I was saved I began to change the way I was living because I wanted to do things the way God would have me do them. I had things in my house like alcohol and a bunch of CD rap music with cussing and I knew that had to go. So Nicole and I took like 100 CD's to the Raider facility and threw them in the dumpster.) He wanted me to know what it really means to be used by God. How God doesn't want us to use our positions and our titles to manipulate our way into a position in His kingdom. He showed me how you have to follow His steps and His process of breaking your heart. That whole December of 1998 God started taking me through a lot. I was on my face before Him and He was dealing with my heart.

Then 1999 rolled around and God opened doors for me to preach at different churches; I was still trying to find my identity. I knew God was saying He was calling me to the ministry. I know I'm licensed to preach, and now I wanted to know what it was that God was saying about who I am?

Then in February of 1999 I was at this church in Salinas, California. I was preaching, and the spirit of God was moving and we had a great service. Then after the meeting the next thing I knew a woman came up to me and said, "Son, when you were up there preaching I saw in red letters over the top of your head 'PROPHET.' God's calling you to be a prophet." She continues on about how God is calling me to be a prophet of the Lord. Then she said this, "God says for you not to get off that football field yet."

Things were beginning to happen at an accelerated pace!

1 Peter 2:9

"But you are a chosen people, a royal priesthood, a holy nation, a people belonging to God, so that you may declare the praises of him who called you out of darkness into his wonderful light."

Romans 12:6

"We have different gifts, according to the grace given us. If a man's gift is prophesying, let him use it in proportion to his faith."

Matthew 10:41

"Anyone who receives a prophet because he is a prophet will receive a prophets reward . . ."

Psalm 105:15

"Do not touch my anointed ones; do my prophets no harm."

Acts 10:43

"All the prophets testify about him that everyone who believes in him receives forgiveness of sins through his name."

2 Peter 1:19

"And we have the word of the prophets made more certain, and you will do well
to pay attention to it, as to a light shining in a dark place, until the day dawns and the
morning star arises in your heart."

Chapter 11

The Move Continues

For a young man who had only a few years prior received God into his heart as Savior and Lord some amazing things were beginning to take place. Napoleon stayed faithful in his dealings with God, and God was faithful in dealing with him. He was open to everything God was sending his way, but still he was cautious and was careful to seek the face of Jesus before each move.

It was an exciting time, one that had Napoleon waking up each day wondering what the Lord had in store for him that day. He now had two healthy little sons. Napoleon IV and Nathaniel and they were the apple of their daddy's eye. They could also keep Nicole hopping.

Football and the nagging injuries had not made the previous year one of Napoleon's favorites but as always he would later realize that this too was all part of God's master plan for his life.

Many times God will bring things into our lives just for the purpose of getting our attention so He can get something across to us. Maybe it's something He wants to change in our life, maybe something he wants us to get involved in, or maybe a major change of direction in our life. And he may use people or situations to do it. We must be open to what He wants.

In Napoleon's case it was a combination of a number of people being sent into his life by God, one confirming what the others had said, regarding his call to the full time ministry. And the situation with football where the injuries he was sustaining and the role he was now playing with the Raiders along with the new contract that Al Davis had given him with the escape clause that would not require Napoleon to pay back his signing bonus. When you add all of this up over a period of several years you see that God had orchestrated each beautiful note in this melody and now Napoleon had to make a choice.

Let's let Napoleon continue this story of his calling as a prophet of God.

A GLIMPSE AT NAPOLEON'S HEART:

1999 was the first year that Tyrone Wheatly came to the Raiders and it was also about that time that God started to deal with me about being selfish. I'm telling you, God really dealt with me!

I had always been the number one guy and here all of a sudden I'm Tyrone's backup. That took some getting use to. It was a tough year in football with the injuries and all, but in my Christian growth things were moving along wonderfully. As I gave it to the Lord I began to see the lesson that He had for me. It was not only for my growth as a Christian, but it somehow brought Tyrone and me closer together and I was able to see God working in his life. Praise god! I did have to deal with the fact that God was taking away some of those things that I had held onto for so long even after I was saved. The reality of the call from God on my life was starting to set in.

When 2000 came around I signed the players contract with Oakland that the brother in Fresno had prophesied to me about, and I had a clause in that contract that stated that after one year, if I wanted to retire and go into the ministry I could do so and would not have to pay back any of my signing bonus. That was amazing! I appreciate Mr. Al Davis, managing general partner of the Raiders for not only doing that, but for all of the support he gave me over the years that I was with the team. I continued to play for the entire year of 2000 but was starting to feel that the days were numbered.

Even though my football stats were not what I had hoped they might be, other things were going great in my life. On September

12th I was ordained to the five- fold ministry of the calling of a prophet. That was a very exciting time for Nicole and me.

I spoke by phone one day with Pastor Cannastraci and we agreed that it was time for me to be ordained to preach. It wasn't long after that that I preached my first sermon in that church on fathers day of 2000 and the Lord moved me to prophecy about the "School of Ministry."

I kept hearing "the school of ministry. The school of ministry." I said, "Why am I hearing something about the school of ministry in my mike? And then suddenly I just started prophesying about the school of ministry there in our church. Now remember that was a Sunday. What I didn't know was that on Friday, all of the pastoral staff had a meeting about what they were going to do with the school of ministry since the man who was running it was leaving to start a church in Virginia, and they were asking God if they should keep the program or let it go.

They were praying for direction and then the first time I had ever preached in our church I started prophesying about the school of ministry! The pastoral staff was awe struck!

Nicole and I were ordained to preach in September of 2000. But there was one more thing that happened to verify that God's hand was in all of this. At the end of the season I took about two months off and I fasted and just consecrated myself before God, asking Him to lay a foundation for my ministry. I was doing paper work, filing, calling pastors back about preaching dates, just tending to the day- to-day business of running a ministry.

Then it happened. I woke up, wide awake about five o'clock in the morning and I felt that God was telling me to retire. I woke my wife up and said, "Honey, I think God wants us to retire. How do you feel?"

Remember it's five o'clock in the morning. She said, " What ever God has for us is what I want."

I told her that that morning the Raiders had an organized team activity, so I'm going to go down there to see if my hearts still in the game. So I went down and practiced with the team and had a wonderful time with the guys. Then when Jon Gruden got up and started writing the X's and O's on the black-

board, I just knew for sure! My time was near.

I went out and had a great day of practice. I mean I was putting moves on people, and my knee felt really good! I had injured it the previous season. But now I felt like my old self out three . . . but my heart was just not in the game anymore. So I came home and told Nicole, "Honey, I felt great out there, but my heart isn't in it anymore. But I'm going back out tomorrow."

But the next day was the same thing. On Wednesday I called Bruce Allen, Raiders senior assistant and told him, "Bruce, I'm going to retire." They already knew that it was just a matter of time. The Raiders were in the middle of a big law suit against the National Football League in Los Angeles and Al Davis was about to take the witness *stand so Bruce asked me if I would wait a few days before making the announcement so I wouldn't upset anyone. I said "No problem."*

That Thursday I went to breakfast with a friend, and I started sharing with him about what I had just done. He looked at me and said, "Brother, in the next couple of days God is going to confirm what you just did."

I didn't give it much thought to what he said at the time. But then on Sunday I was scheduled to preach in a church in San Leandro, California. I was at the church speaking with the pastor, when he told me that when God had called him he had plans to become a professional golfer. Needless to say he was very supportive.

It was that day I went out and preached a message entitled, "Leaving a Legacy." Man, what a response! A lot of people were saved. I don't know how many, but there was a big number.

As I was leaving the building on the way to my car a fellow came up to me to say, "Brother I don't know you. I'm not into professional sports. I'm just not into that stuff. I'm in charge of a group of over 100 people that have pray for the pastor of this church." He told me that that morning as he was getting ready for church the Lord had told him to tell me that He's calling me to the full- time ministry. He said "When I saw you up there preaching, I saw the Lord speaking through you, and the fire of God going into these people. God is calling you into full- time ministry." Three days previously at breakfast my friend had said, "In a couple of days God will confirm what you just did." Praise God!

That following Tuesday I called my agent, Cameron Foster and said "I'm retiring to go into what God is telling me to do."

What to do next? God was giving me a vision and starting to unfold it before me. I felt like one does when writing a book—— I had in mind what I waned to say and what I wanted to get across and suddenly there comes the reality of it all! I can now see clearly things that God had shown me a long time ago, and it was so neat to see it unfold now right before my eyes and in my heart!

THE BIBLE TELLS US:

"Now I know I must listen even closer to the Masters voice. God wants us to be wise stewards of our time and resources. We can't water down the Gospel. He's not going to trust us with these people if we're not going to give them the truth!

Chapter 12

The Real Beginning

April 12, 2001; According to a statement released by Napoleon Kaufman's agent, Cameron Foster, the six - year pro was retiring "to spend more time with his wife, their children, the community and his ministry."

With that simple statement it was now a reality. Napoleon Kaufman, who throughout his entire life had been known as a sensational football player from Pop Warner to the Oakland Raiders of the NFL, would now be known as a servant of God.

Raiders senior assistant, Bruce Allen said the team respects Napoleon's decision but that they also will allow him the latitude to change his mind if he so desires in the future.

In an article by Jerry McDonald in the *Herald* Allen was quoted as saying, "He's talked about this for a couple of years, really. We've been talking more about it in the last few weeks and he feels at this time he that wants to do this."

There it was! Napoleon Kaufman is retired! Even though many of his fans had heard him talk about retiring and about his passion for the Christian ministry it may still have come as a shock to them.

It would seem that the steps we've seen and described here have been ordered by God, and Napoleon has been faithful to proceed as God directed. He knew he would devote full - time to his Crucified with Christ Ministries and that he would continue to travel around preaching wherever God would have him go.

It has been a short and exciting life for this remarkable young man who has seen it all, from the dredges of poverty to the riches and fame as a star professional football player.

God has been gracious with this special young man all along the way of preparation for what He has in store for him by bringing people into his life like Ron Mau, Dick Barrett, Al Lavan, Jerone Davison, David Cannastraci, and a loving wife Nicole who have been there for him throughout his life.

God is that way! He seems to know just what we need or who we need to help us even when we can't see or understand the why. It's easy to ask why? Why does life have to be so difficult? Why can't it all be a bed of roses?

I can't begin to explain all the whys because people having been asking why from the beginning of time and no one has been able to give an answer that pleases us yet. Wouldn't it been just as easy for God to make us all beautiful, healthy, and wealthy? It would in my way of thinking! Like that great line from *The Fiddler on the Roof*, "Would it spoil some vast eternal plan if I were a rich man?" Another question for the Lord when we get to heaven.

But each step of learning, each new accomplishment usually comes from a not so fun position. Learning to walk as a toddler means you will tumble more than once before you get it down and take the next step and run. Getting out of bed, and going to school, so you can get an education that will take you through your life is not the easiest thing to do for a fourteen year old. Going to that same old boring job as a young adult may be the last thing you would like to do but it's all part of the learning process.

Napoleon faced some challenges in his young life that most of us cannot even compute in our minds because we don't have the data. But it always seems when God has a special calling on your life he always seems to have a special boot camp for you.

When we look at the lives of people from the bible we don't have to look much further than the life of Joseph, son of Jacob in the Old Testament, until we see a special young man who is sold into slavery by his own brothers. After he's made the best of that bad situation he's falsely accused and placed in prison for seven years. But God had a plan for him and that plan would eventually play a major part in the history of God's people.

Joseph not only overcame the adversity but he thrived on it, his faith grew. He was elevated to a position that chances are he would never had reached without the trials. He would go on to become the Governor of all Egypt, second in command only to Pharaoh.

All of us, the great and the small will have adversity in our lives and God has a wonderful plan for our lives.. It has always been that way. It's how we deal with adversity that causes our character to develop. For some of us it's easier than others. Some just never seem to get it and continue the fight throughout their lives. They blame others or make excuses. It's true, we can become bitter or better from average circumstances.

Surrender to the Lord is the answer. No one is going to please God unless he determines to surrender his will to that of God's. Being ready to meet every challenge that is thrown our way, knowing that some how, some way God will use this for our good is the only way we will be able to overcome. Now that's hard to do unless you have confidence in the character of God, His love, mercy and His perfect plan for your life.

It's hard to keep from stealing that pair of Nikes when all of the other kids are wearing them and the old generic ones you're wearing have holes, without the assurance that God wants you to prosper with hard work and self-discipline. Taking that shinny bike is a tempting when you are the only one walking unless you know the consequences of stealing are even more painful. But you have got to learn to resist those temptations, and it's not possible without staying in the Word, prayer and an accountability to a group of other Christians. Life is hard, but God is good and will help you through the power of His Holy Spirit to overcome any temptation..

People learn to handle temptation from different ways. Some learn it from godly instruction from parents in the home.

Others learn it the hard way by giving into it and stealing, then getting caught and having to pay the price.

I'm sure there were times in Napoleon's life that he wondered why he couldn't seem to learn the lessons without so much misery. Life's that way. We all hope our children will just walk upright and live by the Ten Commandments but that just doesn't happen very often if ever. But with godly instruction it can be easier to resist temptation.

The one thing that was true in Napoleons life is true in all our lives and that's the call of God. Napoleon was special, but so are all of God's children special. Just as Napoleon felt that tug or call on his life from God, God is calling us all. It's just some of us answer that call sooner than others without having to go through some of the tough times. No one will ever live a trouble free life. If we didn't have problems and trials we would never grow and be usable by the Master.

When Napoleon finally surrendered to Jesus and said "I'm yours, do as you will with my life" only then was he able to be used greatly by God and his ministry, Crucified with Christ Ministries. That work is just now blossoming into something that God can and will use for his glory for years to come.

The things that God is doing in Napoleon's life is just amazing. He is preaching where and when the doors are open and that is usually two or three times per week. The tape ministry is growing and there is talk of a teaching television program.

Napoleon is careful to take every offer, every potential opportunity to God in prayer and God is continuing to bring wise mentors into his life.

When Napoleon made the decision to retire from pro football many people thought, "Wow", look what he's giving up, all that money, fame and glory. He doesn't see it that way at all. He is in wonderment that the people don't see what he's gaining. He doesn't put the money, fame and glory on the same scale with eternal life with a Father who loves him to no end.

Napoleon just prays that each of you readers has decided to surrender to Jesus. His hope is that you will heed the tug and ask God to come into your life as Savior and Friend.

I pray the same for you and also ask that you remember this young man who only wants to please God in your prayers.

THE BIBLE TELLS US:

Mark 16:15

He said to them, " Go into all the world and preach the good news to all creation."

Chapter 13

Things They Said

Bill Soliday <u>Oakland Tribune Writer</u> "Napoleon Kaufman is anything but simplicity in motion. He darts, dips, changes direction, skitters by tacklers and leaves mouths agape. He likes to keep the business of running the ball simple."

Greg McMackin <u>Seattle Seahawks Defensive Coordinator</u> " He's such a great athlete. He can break out on you at any time. He breaks tackles, but he's fast enough to make the big plays."

Joe Bugel <u>Oakland Raider Head Football Coach 1997</u> "Napoleon Kaufman is a class act! He deserves to get the football. He's Mr. Excitement!

Desmond Howard Raider Teammate "For some people to judge Napoleon by his size shows how ignorant they are about the game. I see a talented guy. I don't really see a small guy! I see a guy who wore number 8 at the University of Washington and tore it up every time he touched the ball."

Dick Barrett <u>Lompoc High School Football Coach</u> " He is very special."

Tommy Thompson <u>49er Punter 1996</u> Thompson played on the Pop Warner team in Lompoc with Napoleon and he recalls a special rule that Coach Ron Mau instituted. "Whenever Napoleon got around the end, we'd take a knee—-so we wouldn't get a clipping penalty. There was no reason to clip anyone because nobody was going to catch him. Once he got into the open field no one ever caught him."

Rick Alvord _Valley Daily News_ "Running the football comes easy to Kaufman, like politics to Bill Clinton and singing to Sinatra."

Carl Steward <u>Oakland Tribune Sports Writer</u> "All Nap needs is a crack and he's in the next county as he showed us on a 70-yard run against the then defending Super Bowl Champs, the Green Bay Packers."

Jerone Davison <u>Raider Team Mate</u> (On NK) "The Bible talks about fruit coming to full maturity. Our fruit is those we bring to God, and I see my fruit flourishing- and that makes me feel good."

Ron Mau <u>Napoleon's Pop Warner Coach</u> "When I saw him I just knew he was going to do something, sports, acting, or singing, I just knew he was special."

Kent Elola <u>Watsonville Register Sports Writer</u> "Napoleon Kaufman is a man with a boys smile,

Joe Bugel <u>Raiders Head Football Coach 1997</u> : He (NK) has the ability to go the distance on every play. He's a very, very explosive back"

Mario Murillo <u>Christian evangelist and Friend</u> What he (NK) does to the Devil is just as potent as what he does to NFL defenders."

Kevin Gilbride <u>San Diego Chargers Coach</u> "He's just performed brilliantly. He's a great football player."

Pat Harlow <u>Raider Tackle</u> "He gets lost back there. He gets behind Wiz and center Barret Robbins and all of a sudden he's in your face. And if he's in your face he's probably already by you. If that kid hits the hole and gets to the linebacker level without being hit he could literally go every time."

Steve Wisniewski <u>Raider Offensive Lineman</u> "Its fun to see those long runs. It takes the steam out of the defense."

Monte Poole <u>San Francisco Chronicle Writer</u> " Napoleon has been compared to the great Detroit Lions running back, Barry Sanders. They both have magical moves, and they're legitimate scoring threats every time they get by that initial wave of defenders."

Jon Gruden <u>Raiders Head Football Coach</u> "I think when he (NK) gets a chance to play and to get into a rhythm, you are going to see Napoleon have some big hits. He's that type of guy."

David Bush <u>San Francisco Chronicle Sports Writer</u> " Napoleon Kaufman earns his money carrying the football and spends his passion carrying The Word."

Ray Perkins <u>Raiders Offensive Coordinator</u> "With Napoleon, there have been times when teams have been in perfect defenses but he just outran them or made a great cut. You can't defend that. Its something special!"

Steve Wisniewski <u>Raider Offensive Lineman</u> "He makes ordinary runs seem spectacular. It looks like up the middle and a cloud of dust, but he breaks them. It looks like 2 or 3 yards and he's hitting it for 40-50 yards. He reminds me very much of my days blocking for Bo Jackson."

Darrell Russell <u>Raider Defensive Lineman</u> (Referring to when his USC Trojans took on the Washington Huskies while they were in college.) "I didn't tackle him, but I made an attempt. You can say you put some hits on him and try to take him out of the game, but he's very powerful. He can take a beating. That's the problem for defenders."

Mike White <u>Raider Head Football Coach 1995-96</u> " He is a guy who is going to do the unexpected. He's a crowd pleaser."

Neil Hayes <u>Contra Costa Times Writer</u> "When he's not breaking a long run he's threatening to run back a kick off for a touchdown."

Jon Gruden <u>Raider Head Coach</u> " I think he's (NK) the greatest open-field back in football. His explosiveness, his creativity, his play-making ability, is such a huge part of our offense."

Jim Jenkins <u>Bee Staff Writer</u> "Crowds react with excitement whenever the ball is in his (NK) hands, and opposing coaches see him as a unique talent."

Joe Bugel <u>Raider Head Football Coach 1997</u> "He runs with great explosion."

Mel Kiper Jr. *1995 Draft Report* "He (NK) will also prove to be a tremendous boost in the locker room. His energy and contagious spirit will be an added bonus."

Bobby Ross San Diego Chargers Head Coach "He's very dangerous. He finds creases, with speed to step inside or go outside."

Bill Soliday Staff Writer "You say you're weary of athletes who think the world owes them something, who are convinced they get no respect and deserve a larger share of the pie? Then you'll love Napoleon Kaufman, the Raiders will'o the wisp tailback."

Mike White Raiders Head football Coach 1995-96 " I've been impressed with him since he's (NK) been here. He hasn't been selfish. For his age and years in the league, I see a very mature guy."

Billy Joe Hobert UofW Teammate "My wife said, even when he gains one yard, he's fun to watch. He's just sooo quick."

Glenn Dickey San Francisco Chronicle Writer "When he's (NK) in the game, the defense always has to be aware of his special ability, which changes the way they play."

Dick Barrett Lompoc HS Head Football Coach " Nip, kept his focus. When he puts his mind to something he really goes after it."

Jon Gruden Raiders Head Coach "When I saw him (NK) with his shirt off, it was Superman. He looks like Baby Hulk, just not green."

Neil Hayes <u>C.C. Times Writer</u> "Catching him (NK) is like trying to catch a flat stone as it skips wildly across a small pond. He's perpetually in fast-forward."

Bishop Harris <u>Raiders Running Back Coach</u> "So many things come natural to him."

Joe Buchsbaum *Pro Football Weekly* "(NK) Is a legitimate home run—-breakaway threat."

Bryan Cox <u>Chicago Bear Linebacker</u> " He's explosive. He hits the hole, and there aren't many (defensive) guys in the league with that kind of speed. . . You have to get lots of hats on him whenever he touches the ball."

Greg Skrepenak <u>Raider Offensive Tackle</u> "He (NK) gives us more weapons."

Jeff Woodruff <u>UW offensive coordinator</u> "Napoleon played in more big games as a freshman and sophomore than a lot of running backs play in their whole careers—-two Rose Bowls and a whole lot of games on national television."

Jim Lambright <u>UW Head Football Coach</u> " He's as durable as they come."

Barbara Hedges <u>UW Athletic Director</u> "He's a beauty."

Blaine Newham <u>Seattle Times</u> "Kaufman moved through a good Cal defense like a crab trying to avoid the boiling pot."

Jeff Hostetler <u>Former Raider Quarterback</u> "He hides behind linemen and all of a sudden he squirts up the sideline and nobody catches him."

Al Lavan <u>UofW Running Backs Coach</u> "The first time I saw him run for the end zone I said, "Wow, he reminds me of Tony Dorsett." (Lavan had been Hall of Famer Dorsett's coach with the Dallas Cowboys.)

Nicole Kaufman <u>Napoleon's wife</u> "He didn't have a romantic bone in his body."

"NAP TIME"

HOW ABOUT A FEW COMMENTS MADE BY NAPOLEON OVER THE YEARS?

"When they call my number in the huddle I just run."

"I'm probably my worst critic. I'm always looking to get better."

"I feel like whenever I get the ball I want to score a touchdown. I've felt that way since I was seven years old and I will continue to feel that way."

"I've been playing this game a long time, I don't get frustrated."

(On the prayer sessions with Jerone Davison in their training camp room) "Sometimes we're in there praying so hard that people think we're fighting. But we're just calling out to God. We need strength man. We need strength!"

"This game isn't that complicated. I just get the ball and run with it like I've done since I was a little kid."

"It's great to wear the purple and gold again."

"I consider myself a warrior."

"I'll even cheerlead."

"If you go back and watch my tapes in high school and college, I'm always running up the middle. I haven't anything to prove as far as running up the middle."

"They call it. We haul it!"

" I try to watch film as much as I can. I'll look at what I did to see if can do things better."

"I run the same plays that everyone else does. It isn't like they have plays designed especially for me."

*"I just run. A lot of people have doubts and I just continue to run . .
"I don't think those (durability) questions will ever vanish. People will always see me as a smaller back."*

(Speaking of his early days in Peewee football) They'd pitch the ball to me and if there was nowhere to go I'd just run out of bounds. I didn't have any moves back then."

"I'll miss the fans. I love the fans."

The fans will miss you Napoleon!